'Everyone has a story. As Bill shares his own personal story of interacting with God and learning to be present in the presence of God, it is a reminder that our God is ever so personal and loves to interact with his children. When it comes to the gift of prophesy, it is often the most messy, as well as confusing to many who are trying to understand how and why the gift exists. Far too often pastors tend to be wary of what the prophetic can involve. But, as Bill points out in, if we just break down the Scriptures and take a close look into our everyday life, we can clearly see the gift of prophecy is simply just learning to be present in the presence of God. It makes so much sense as to why the Apostle Paul desired that each and every one of us would learn to live with this gift as a natural by-product of our everyday life, as in doing so it benefits all. As you read Bill's story, I pray it encourages you in your own walk with God knowing that not only does God want to talk with you, but that he also loves and desires to talk through you so that you will encourage and build up those Gods sends along your path.'

Christy Wimber, author, former TV Host on TBN, and CBN, former Head Pastor of a Vineyard Church.

'A deeply moving invitation to tune into "that gentle whisper" from the heart of God. Bill invites us to take seriously God's gifts of prophecy, words of knowledge, visions and dreams. Full of poignant personal stories, he self-effacingly offers a map for using keys of love and faith to convey God's gentle whispers to unlock deep treasure, buried all around us, in the lives of friends and strangers. A taste of the conversation at the heavenly banquet! I read it in tears.'

Rt Revd Dr Jill Duff, Anglican Bishop of Lancaster.

that
gentle
whisper

Bill Cahusac / *Foreword by Pete Greig*

that *gentle* whisper

LEARNING TO RECOGNISE
GOD'S VOICE IN A NOISY WORLD

Muddy
Pearl

Published in 2021 by
Muddy Pearl, Edinburgh, Scotland.
www.muddypearl.com
books@muddypearl.com

British Library Cataloguing in Publication Data

A catalogue record for this book is available from the British Library

HB ISBN 978-1-914553-05-9
PB ISBN 978-1-914553-01-1

Typeset in Minion by Revo Creative Ltd, Lancaster

Printed in Great Britain by Bell & Bain Ltd, Glasgow

*To Nici. Who inspires me every day
with the way she runs her race.*

foreword

The Canadian Sugar Maple is a show-off of a tree. Flaunting its flaming red flowers in the autumn, oozing that sweet sap we call maple syrup, it's about as pretty and sweet as a tree can be, but *beware! Don't be fooled!* The Sugar Maple has one of the shallowest root systems of any tree anywhere in the world. With so much on show, but just ten to twenty centimetres beneath the surface, it's as shallow as a tree can be. One careless sneeze and it's firewood.

At the other end of the arboreal spectrum there's the Shepherd Tree of the Kalahari Desert, which has the deepest root system on earth. Reaching down seventy metres – one hundred times deeper than the Sugar Maple – the Shepherd Tree can survive some of the harshest conditions on the planet.

In a world of Sugar Maples, my friend Bill Cahusac has the depth and strength of a Shepherd Tree. He has remained faithful, fruitful and kind, standing strong through many trials. One fruit of that deep-rootedness is Bill's exceptional prophetic gift, drawn up from the deep and secret places of his relationship with Jesus. He has often brought God's word powerfully to me personally, to our church family, and to the wider 24-7 movement. In fact, he won't like me telling you this, but Bill hears God in ways I don't. He receives remarkably accurate words of knowledge, has encountered angels, and seems to be able to crack entire meetings open with a single prophetic insight. As you read this book you're going to be amazed by the stories he recounts, but there is also much that he hasn't shared, simply I suspect out of humility.

By now you may be picturing a wild-eyed mystic but Bill is nothing of the sort. He laughs until tears roll down his cheeks, knows more about movies than most people, loves sport, prioritises his family, and deals each day with the real, gritty, earthy stuff of pastoral ministry – from constructing coffee rotas to conducting funerals. Bill Cahusac is the real deal.

Some people with Bill's level of prophetic gifting would use it to build high-profile ministries for themselves, but he isn't interested in that sort of thing (I've tried to persuade him and he just says 'no!'). Instead, he has chosen to belong to a team, to be rooted in place and time, to quietly help build a community that looks a lot like Jesus. This is why he has written this book, in line with the Apostle Paul's teaching that:

> Christ himself gave … the prophets … to equip his people for works of service, so that the body of Christ may be built up.
> EPHESIANS 4:11–12

The material in this book began as a series of popular workshops run by Bill for members of Emmaus Rd Church. In other words, it's tried, tested and rooted in the real experiences of a living local church. My prayer therefore is that it will help you to put down your own deep roots like the Shepherd Tree, by equipping you practically not just to prophesy on Sunday morning, but to wake up on Monday morning familiar with *that gentle whisper*.

Pete Greig

PETE GREIG
24-7 PRAYER INTERNATIONAL
Emmaus Rd Church, Guildford, UK
June 2021

no expert

'What have you got to lose?'

I wasn't entirely sure if it was a question or a statement, but off the top of my head I could think of a couple of things: my reputation and being misunderstood for starters.

I had been toing and froing about writing this book for months. I had only told three people about the opportunity: Nici, Pete, and my closest friend Piers. They had all encouraged me, but I was still unsure. Stephanie, the publisher, had been more than patient with me as I considered whether writing a book was something I really wanted to do. What I didn't want to do was say yes and then change my mind, or waste anymore of anyone's time. I knew I actually needed to decide one way or the other.

If I was going to write a book, I wanted it to be authentic and honest. In short it meant being vulnerable. That involved a willingness to commit my own journey, warts and all, to paper, and I wasn't sure how up for that I actually was.

I didn't say much, because what my friend didn't know was that those six words were far more to me than just a bit of friendly encouragement. They were the answer to many hours of wondering, wrestling and countless prayers culminating in a request, 'Lord, I don't care how you speak, but I need you to speak to me about this.' And when I least expected it, it happened; I had my answer. It was that gentle whisper once again, this time speaking through a friend who, as is often the way, was totally oblivious to the fact that God had just spoken through her.

My biggest worry was what people were going to think. Particularly friends who don't have the same perspective – or have a faith that is more traditional.

'I think you're overthinking it,' said our friend. 'I wouldn't worry too much – most of them won't read it anyway. What's the worst that could happen?'

If you have picked up this book in the hope of learning from an expert, you should probably put it back on the shelf now.

This book began its life as a course I wrote and taught at our church in Guildford, mostly so that I could remind myself of some of the things I have begun to learn in the last thirty years.

As will become apparent, it has never been my intention to write a textbook or workbook where I pass on the techniques I have picked up over the years. This is more of a memoir of sorts, where I have shared some stories and insights I have gained, and the lessons that I continue to learn along the way. Each chapter follows on from the next, and, I hope, builds on what we explore in a way that might give us some insight into how we might grow in the prophetic.

The prophetic can be both the most extraordinary gift to the church, and also the cause of some church leaders' greatest anxiety – and I write that as someone who calls it one of the greatest joys in my life to pastor a church in Guildford! It is my hope that in reading this book you will be encouraged, will know that God loves you, is closer than you think and that, if you let him, he will draw you into a friendship with him that will bring huge blessing to your life, and those you meet.

I have been as honest as I can in sharing the stories that I have. There are times when I have been left in awe by what God can do, and others when I have been left exasperated by my own mistakes.

It may sound somewhat corny, but I think, wherever you are on your journey, that we are all pilgrims, on a boat, searching for the shore. Searching for that place where we can find home, safety and intimacy with the one who has known and loved us since before the beginning of time. It is my hope that these pages will encourage you that the shore beckons, even from a distance, and that home is perhaps closer than we think.

acknowledgements

Thank you:

They say it takes a village to raise a child. The same is true of a book! So much of what I've shared in these pages is the result of many people walking with me over many years.

These are just some who have shaped my story and encouraged me along the way.

Mum – you are nothing short of extraordinary. In every way. Although I don't talk about you much in this book, you taught me so much about loving people and seeing the best in them. In that sense, your example helped write every page.

Sandy and Annette Millar – someone asked me recently what I learned about hearing God's voice and ministry in the Spirit from you. My response was 'everything I know'. You modelled to me what it is to love and serve a church family. You are forerunners and heroes.

Nicky and Pippa Gumbel – you have loved and encouraged me since I first walked through the doors at Holy Trinity Brompton as a slightly bemused and very over-dressed sixteen-year-old. You cheered me on as I grew and stepped out, and then invited Nici and I back onto the staff team when I needed a safe place to heal. You trusted me to share what I felt God was saying in staff meetings and then in church services, even when it meant they ran slightly over. I will be forever thankful for your kindness and belief in me.

To the many friends who have journeyed with me over the years and encouraged me to dare to believe that that gentle whisper just might be God – in particular Tim, Sarah, Katie, Olly, Emily, Wayne, Wendy, Miles, Sarah, Martyn, Emily, Jonny, Tara, Ben, Jules, Frog, Amy, Mark, Margeaux, Clare, and Mark.

To those older and wiser prophetic voices who have so often provided sage advice when I needed it – Piers Jennings, Jeremy Jennings, Ric and

Louie Thorpe, Adam Atkinson, Alex and Rebecca Stewart, Giles Inglis-Jones, Ken Costa, Graham Tomlin, John and Annie Hughes, Mark Wagner, Carl Wills, Christine and Craig Westhoff, Tim and Dhana Wimberly, and Patrick and Philly Pearson Miles.

· This book began its life as a course we ran at Emmaus Rd Church. Each time we ran the course the feedback we received from those who came along helped to continue to shape it. Thank you to each and every one of the people who gave up their evenings to come and explore how we might learn to recognise God's voice in a noisy world. Your humour, encouragement, enthusiasm, and patience inspired me to keep working on the material. Particular thanks to Joanna Callender who acted both as a sounding board for ideas and also unofficial course content editor (and sometimes course corrector). Thanks too to the whole staff and Elders teams at Emmaus Rd who constantly cheered me on when I wasn't sure if I should run the course or not, and to the wider Emmaus Rd and 24-7 Prayer family – I love being part of this wild and crazy tribe. To Pete and Sammy Grieg in particular, who gave me space to grow and wings to fly.

To the many friends that cheered me on and encouraged me during the writing of this book – you know who you are. Thank you.

To Stephanie, who somehow managed to turn my at times incoherent manuscript into what you are now reading. You really are nothing short of a genius – thank you to you and the whole Muddy Pearl team for taking a risk on me. To Hannah Heather and the numerous other readers who took the time to read the manuscript with such diligence.

Finally, to Nici, Luke, Jonah, and Zach – for loving me, believing in me, keeping my feet on the ground, reminding me to keep it real and making anywhere you are my favourite place. I love you more than words can say. x

contents

home

How lovely is your dwelling place,
  LORD Almighty!
My soul yearns, even faints,
  for the courts of the LORD;
my heart and my flesh cry out
  for the living God.

PSALM 84:1–2

He was standing at the back of the church with his arms folded – he looked like he'd rather be pretty much anywhere else, which struck me as strange because he was on his own and the event was one that guests had to book to attend.

Whenever I see someone who is disengaged at the back of a church meeting, it catches my attention, it's the equivalent of a red flag. It just reminds me of myself so many years ago. I began thinking and praying, 'Lord, what's the way in here? How can this be a win for him?' My next prayer was, 'Lord, please give me a way in – his name, anything.'

As I asked, I had a deep conviction, a knowing, that he was called John. Which also seemed like a pretty safe bet, as half the people in the room were men, so there was almost certainly going to be a John. I took a breath and walked up to him.

'Hi, are you John?' I enquired, my heart beating slightly faster than usual. It didn't feel like a huge risk, asking him, mainly because if I had been wrong, I could have just apologised and moved the conversation on fairly naturally.

'Yes, I am,' he replied.

'Hi, I'm Bill,' I said, holding out my hand and offering him a handshake.

'Lord, what matters to him?' I prayed silently as we shook hands.

'*Football.*'

'Football?' I replied silently. 'Really?'

'*Really. And it really matters to him.*'

I paused. It didn't feel like too much of a leap of faith for football to mean something to him – football meant something to lots of people. I know faith is supposed to be slightly more certain than quietly considering the odds, but for me, my faith is often built in those moments by remembering the previous step, which in this case had been that there was a man called John in the room … if he was called John, it gave me more faith that I was encountering the voice of God, and that football mattered to him.

'Is football important to you?' I asked.

'Villa all the way!' he replied.

'That's fine, as long as you are happy with Fulham being God's favourites,' I smiled.

'Frankly, you need all the help you can get!' John called back, his arms slightly less folded as we both laughed.

'Thank you, Lord,' I said silently, not just because my faith was continuing to grow, but because actually the banter and a bit of laughter took all the intensity out of the exchange, not just for John, but for both of us.

As I laughed, I had a picture in my mind's eye. I saw a black and white image of a young boy walking towards a football stadium holding an older man's hand. As I allowed the image to play out, I saw it tear apart, and felt a sadness – and at that moment had a knowing.

'I hope you don't mind me asking, but would I be right in saying that it was your father who gave you your love of football? That he used to take you to games?' I asked.

He nodded, and I could feel something shift in the conversation, as if in that moment we had begun to move towards something slightly more personal for him, something that really mattered to him.

'How do I ask this question in a way that doesn't trivially expose his pain?' I thought.

I was aware that what was happening wasn't a game – this man was someone dearly loved by God, whose story mattered to God, and, in that moment, it was no longer about my next step of faith, it was about something deep and personal in this man's life, and God reaching out to him. I could see from the look on his face that what I asked had resonated with him. He swallowed hard.

'And that while you were close when you were a child, your relationship became hard, and it is now not what it once was?'

I could tell from his response that what I had asked had struck a chord with him.

'Yes,' he replied, his voice cracking with emotion. 'We're estranged, and haven't spoken for many years.'

I paused, aware of how vulnerable he had just made himself, and looked him in the eye.

'How do you know all this?' he asked curiously. 'I haven't talked to anyone about this for years.'

'John, although I'm not quite sure you know why you came here tonight,' I said slowly, 'I believe that God is inviting you on a journey of healing with him, not just for you personally, but also in your relationship with your father. To give you the courage to be the one who reaches out, and to help you begin that process of reconciliation that you want, to give you the words to say the things that you don't quite know how to say. I think God wants to encourage you – he loves you, your relationship with your father matters to him, and he will be with you through the whole process.'

John was understandably getting quite emotional now. 'Thank you,' he said quietly, 'I don't really know why I came tonight, and I definitely wasn't expecting anything like this to happen … ' he swallowed back the tears I could see in his eyes. 'This means more than you will ever know,' he said, his voice shaking with emotion.

He shook me by the hand again, I gave him my phone number and told him that if he needed anything, I would be more than happy to help. He thanked me again and said he would be in touch.

It was wonderful to hear from John a few weeks later saying that he and his father had met for the first time in sixteen years, and that while there was still a lot of ground to cover, he was hopeful that over time the relationship could begin to mend.

God is in the business of reaching out to people who arrive at meetings not really knowing why they are there, and beginning the process of healing and reconciliation in relationships.

When I think back, so many of the encounters I have had over the years are like the one with John. They have the same theme, the same thread running through them: relationships matter deeply to God.

If you remember nothing else from this book, remember this: love is the key.

Love in this case is not a soft, mushy, sentimental feeling. Love means being prepared to make yourself vulnerable, to take a risk and reach out, it means being present with someone and sharing what you believe God has put on your heart, or in your mind for them, remembering that what has been revealed to you is sacred and has the power to lead people into an encounter with God that could change the trajectory of their lives.

Now, I'm going to tell you my story.

I was not brought up in a Christian home. My mother was a single parent: my father died of lung cancer when I was three, and my younger brother was one. My family's only connection with religion or faith was that, during the Second World War, my father was evacuated and grew up with his cousin. My father then joined the navy, and his cousin went on to be a church leader during the charismatic renewal in the UK in the 1970s and 1980s. When it became clear that my father was terminally ill, my mother wrote to his cousin and said, 'Please would you come and see him. He's gravely ill.' She received a reply saying he was really busy and that sadly he couldn't visit, but instead he sent a prayer on a card. If you asked my mother what her perspective on faith, and on people of faith, was, well, at best, and if she was being polite, she would have said ambivalent. Probably entirely as a result of that experience.

My grandfather used to go to church and sing in the choir but would leave before the sermon started. He would get up, step out of the choir stall, walk straight down the middle aisle, and out of the church. You can imagine how encouraging that was for whoever was preaching!

My grandmother, who I was very close to, was born in Lancashire in very difficult circumstances – seemingly out of wedlock but adopted quietly by her mother's sister and her husband. She spent much of her time with her unmarried 'aunt' as she grew up, and some of that in 'the poorhouse'. Eventually she became a nurse, working in Liverpool during the Second World War, being lowered down bomb craters to tend to the dying, and witnessing extraordinary pain and suffering. As a consequence of all this, she didn't have much time for anything to do with established religion. She would roll her eyes when my grandfather hummed the hymns he had been singing during the part of the church service he had attended before his aforementioned departure, just before the sermon that Sunday morning.

I grew up in London, in a terraced house in Fulham, with my mother and my brother. We were a close family and the street we lived in was friendly – everyone knew everyone, and people were in and out of each other's houses. When I was fifteen, a family moved in two doors down. They made their mark on the community quickly with their gregarious and fun-loving nature. There was something about this family that was extraordinarily attractive, and the more time I spent with them, the more intrigued I became. There was something about them that I couldn't quite put my finger on, that I hadn't experienced before.

It wasn't just that they were charismatic people, lots of fun to be around and the life and soul of every party. And it wasn't just that they were kind in a way I hadn't encountered before. They had a way of talking about people that was so disarming, even to a fifteen-year-old. I thought nobody could really be that nice and that kind all the time. My experience of people up until that point was that they generally said all the right things in a social setting until someone left, and then would say what they *actually* thought about them, which was often not quite as kind and flattering. But not this family. They always seemed to see the best in others, and to speak well of people. In fact, to my surprise, they were often even more positive and effusive about people *after* they had left the room.

This was so alien to my upbringing, my experience. I had no grid for them; they didn't fit into any box that I had in my head. I didn't know what to make of them – there was something about them that was both incredibly attractive and incredibly confusing, but that I wanted to be around.

But there was something else that I couldn't put my finger on, almost as though they shared a kind of deep secret.

Eventually one afternoon, after I'd helped the mum take the shopping in and been offered a cup of tea, and I was sitting chatting with them and a couple of their friends who were there, they just casually mentioned that they went to church. I was completely thrown by this, it was pretty much the last thing that I expected them to say – I'd never met anyone my age who went to church, much less who was so much fun to be around!

I don't know if you've ever been in a situation like this, where you hear a voice that sounds like yours committing to do something you have no desire to do whatsoever. But there I was, sipping tea, trying to make sense of what they had just said, and before I knew it, I heard a voice that sounded alarmingly like mine say, 'Oh, I'll come to church.'

And the problem is once it's out there you can't really take it back. You can't say, 'Oh only joking, I didn't really mean that.' And without missing a beat one of them said, 'Great, well how about next week?' The truth was that going to church was pretty much the last thing that I wanted to do with them, or anyone else, but I've never been very good at being on the back foot. And so, everything just sort of went into slow motion. I think I nodded and smiled, but the thought that kept running round my head was, 'What. On. Earth. Were. You. Thinking?'

My only experience of church was at boarding school, when we had chapel twice a week and once on a Sunday. Nobody sang the hymns, other than *Jerusalem*, and that was only wheeled out when someone had been expelled, and was sung more as an act of defiance than worship. The sermons were boring, irrelevant and seemed to last an age.

There was a Bible study that someone in my house at school used to run on Tuesday afternoons, and I would do my utmost to disrupt it. I would keep opening the door to the room, or make stupid noises from downstairs, or crash steel dustbin lids together outside the room to make so much noise that no one would have been able to hear anything. One time, I actually managed to turn the circuit breaker for the building off, so that all the lights went off and it was too dark for anyone in the Bible study (or as it turned out, anyone in the building) to read anything at all.

And yet, in a moment of I'm not sure what, I had just volunteered to go to a church service at 6:30pm on a summer evening the following week.

So, on the evening of 24th of June 1990, one of the hottest days of the year, aged sixteen, I put on my school suit, which was grey, hot and itchy, and I put on my tie, polished my shoes, found some cuff links and actually brushed my hair, because in my mind that was what you did when you went to church.

When I rang their doorbell, I was met by people in T-shirts and shorts. Which was a surprise, because I thought we were going to church. Okay, I reasoned to myself, maybe we are going out afterwards somewhere.

We got on the tube, made our way across London, and when we arrived outside the church there was a big garden full of people. I thought there must be something else going on, because this garden was *absolutely full* of people, all my sort of age, some older some younger, some in their twenties and thirties.

Then I noticed that they were all going *into* the church! I'd never seen so many people voluntarily go into a church building at 6:30pm on a Sunday evening, when they could be at home, playing sport or out somewhere having a barbecue with their friends.

The second thing I noticed, although I couldn't quite put my finger on it at the time, was that as I walked through the door, surrounded by people I had never met before, I felt weirdly at home, even though this was pretty much the last place I would have expected or indeed planned to have been a few days before.

The third thing I noticed was that nobody else was wearing a suit. Nobody else was even wearing a jacket. In fact, nobody else was even wearing a smart shirt. Not even the man who later spoke – he was wearing, very sensibly, a polo shirt, because it was hot.

Then the man with the guitar started playing, and then people started waving their hands in the air, and I just stood there, and wondered what on earth was going on. Why, I thought, were people waving their hands around? Was I supposed to raise my hands? I tried to explain it when I got home and the only way I could describe it was that it was a bit like watching people clean the windows. It was such a surreal experience, far from anything I'd experienced before.

It threw up a lot of questions for me. It was a paradigm shift in my experience of church – which up until this point had been, pretty much, just boring.

As I got to know more and more of these people, I was struck by how they all had this same quality that I couldn't quite put my finger on, and I found myself wanting to go back, because there was something strangely compelling about what happened for an hour and fifteen minutes on a Sunday evening. It was the first time in my life that I had met people who talked about Jesus like he was a real person – like they actually knew him. Even when the family who had initially taken me went away on holiday, I found myself going to church by myself.

While I was at a church service, one of the notices was about something called Alpha, which was a course they ran for people who wanted to know a bit more about faith, and so after a bit of encouragement from my neighbours and some of their friends, who had also started to become my friends, I signed up – at least for the first week.

I have to confess that had someone told me at the start of 1990 that by June of that year I would have volunteered to go to church, and that by September I would have signed up for Alpha, I wouldn't have believed them, and yet, even after a last-minute crisis when I asked myself what I was doing, and what my friends would think, I found myself at Alpha, and actually, to my surprise, enjoying it.

The talks were the first I'd ever heard that explained the Christian faith to me in a way that made sense. And when they said that no question was too stupid to ask in the small group discussion, they really did mean it. I really enjoyed the course, and even on the odd occasion half raised one hand during a church service.

Then came the weekend away, the part of the course known at the time as the Holy Spirit weekend. I signed up rather apprehensively, and after another brief 'What. Was. I. Thinking?' moment, along with a quick check as to the nearest railway station in case of a 'family emergency', packed my bags and, armed with the most recent train timetable, headed down to Pontins in Bracklesham Bay, just near Chichester.

The weekend was far less intense than I had worried it might be. The talks were engaging and by the end of the first day I had a better understanding of who the Holy Spirit was, and what he did, than after however many school chapel services and Religious Studies lessons at school. The third session of Saturday was billed as 'How can I be filled with the Holy Spirit?' – the thought of which had got me and my friend Nick looking nervously at the train timetable during a walk on the beach after lunch, before reassuring each other that if it did get too uncomfortable, we could always sneak out and call a taxi to take us to the station.

As it turned out both Nick and I were absolutely glued to our seats. There was none of the weirdness that we had been so worried about, and at the end of the talk when someone asked me if I wanted to be filled with the Holy Spirit, and offered to pray for me, I found myself saying 'sure' without the 'What. Was. I. Thinking?' thought crossing my mind after I'd said yes.

If I'm honest, I didn't really entirely understand what being prayed to be filled with the Holy Spirit actually meant, or what to expect, great talk notwithstanding, but when the person prayed for me, I just felt really peaceful – I was a slightly hyperactive sixteen-year-old, and I just felt this peace wash over me. And that feeling again. The same feeling I had experienced a few months previously when I walked through those church doors for the first time. That feeling of *home*.

A few days later I was on the London Underground somewhere between Goodge Street and Warren Street on the Northern line. I found myself thinking about my neighbours, and their friends, some of whom I now counted as my friends, and I suppose I had what might be described as one of those penny-drop moments. I thought, 'They're Christians. I really like them. I really want to *be* like them … maybe I should become a Christian.'

So, I came to faith, aged sixteen, on the Northern Line, somewhere between Goodge Street and Warren Street. And again, in that moment, the same feeling of being *home*.

Over the last thirty years, what I have come to realise is that what I experienced in the people that I met, and what I experienced the first time I walked into that church, and what I experienced when people prayed for me on that Alpha weekend – that feeling of *home* – was that in those moments, and many since, I had encountered the presence of God.

The presence of God changed everything for me. That's when faith became about a person, not a thing; that's when it became about a living relationship rather than a person in a book. There's nothing, I think, more important for us individually, or the church today, than to take hold of the reality of the presence of God.

Over time I recognised that the thing about my neighbours that made them so compelling and so full of life, was that they carried the presence of God – it was almost as if it radiated from them. When I stepped into the church it was as if it filled the room. When I was prayed for that first time (and many times since), it was as if in some way it was imparted to me.

What I've come to understand is that we were created to know the presence of God, to enjoy the presence of God and to carry the presence of God. And it is the presence of God that makes us distinct.

So, if you've come to this book asking questions like: How do I encounter the presence of God more? How do I learn to encounter his voice more? I want to emphasise from the start that I am no expert. I am just learning, like everybody else. But whatever stage you are at, my hope is that you will grow in your ability to recognise and know the presence of God, be comfortable in the presence of God, and know what to do when you encounter the presence of God. And then, that you will learn how to recognise his voice and how, and also importantly whether to share that with other people and when.

When we look at the Bible, from the very beginning, right back at the start of Genesis, when God created Adam and he created Eve, they walked with him – in his presence – in the cool of the day.

Israel, God's people, were made to know God's presence; they carried his presence in the Ark. Jesus was the embodiment of the presence of God; he was God, present in a person. And then God sends his Holy Spirit, in the book of Acts, to come and fill the people of God, so that they become the tabernacle, the temple of God. And finally, one day, the earth will be full of the glory of the Lord. And, as followers of Jesus, we live with the promise that God's presence will be with us, his people, always.

God's presence is his great invitation, and our great distinction.

I want to take us back to the story of when Moses reads the book of the law to the Israelites and they in turn promise to obey everything they have heard. They enter into a covenant with him.

In our culture it can be hard to understand the importance of this moment, and the importance of covenant. A covenant can be best understood in this context as a legally binding contract between God and his people, which both have entered into voluntarily. It is a huge moment.

It is after this moment that God calls Moses to join him on Mount Sinai, to spend time in his presence, and during this time God will give him tablets of stone, with the commandments and the law that the people of Israel had just covenanted with God to keep, written on them. As Moses ascends the mountain, a cloud hides him from view. We recognise the cloud, in the Bible, as a manifestation of the presence of God. And Moses spends forty days, hidden with God, in his presence.

At the foot of the mountain, the people who only days before had entered into this new covenant with God begin to get restless. Moses has been gone for days and they don't know whether he is alive or dead. It is at this point that they approach Moses' older brother Aaron, who is also their high priest, and ask him to make them new gods to worship. Aaron, for his part, tells them to bring him their gold earrings, which he melts down and makes into an idol in the shape of a calf. 'Here are your gods, Israel, who brought you out of Egypt!' he exclaims.

In many ways this is so hard to fathom. What happened to the zeal they had when they entered into the covenant with God? Do they not remember that it is far more than a gentleman's agreement, easily said, easily broken?

It is at this moment, as they begin to worship these new idols, that God tells Moses to go down the mountain, as the people have already begun to worship new gods. And as Moses leaves the presence of God and descends the mountain, he sees what is happening. He throws down the two stone tablets with the law of God and the commandments written on them, the law and the covenant that only forty days ago they had promised to keep, and they are broken to pieces, much like the covenant they have broken.

Then the LORD said to Moses, 'Leave this place, you and the people you brought up out of Egypt, and go up to the land I promised on oath to Abraham, Isaac and Jacob, saying, "I will give it to your descendants." I will send an angel before you and drive out the Canaanites, Amorites, Hittites, Perizzites, Hivites and Jebusites. Go up to the land flowing with milk and honey. But I will not go with you, because you are a stiff-necked people and I might destroy you on the way.'

EXODUS 33:1–3

They have been on a journey to the home that God has for them, this land flowing with milk and honey, and he says, 'You can go, it's all yours – but I am not going with you.' You can almost hear a collective gasp and shock when God says, 'You go, but I am not going with you.'

And their response is this:

When the people heard these distressing words, they began to mourn.
EXODUS 33:4

Their response is fascinating: they mourn. He's promising the very thing that they have been on this journey for. He says, 'It's yours, have it!' But they are mourning because he is not going with them. All the other things that were promised are nothing compared to his presence being with them.

And a little while later, Moses says this:

'If your Presence does not go with us, do not send us up from here. How will anyone know that you are pleased with me and with your people unless you go with us? What else will distinguish me and your people from all the other people on the face of the earth?'
EXODUS 33:15-16

His presence is not the means by which we experience an encounter and take hold of everything else; his presence is the end itself. Knowing his presence, encountering his presence, being in his presence – is the end. Just as in the beginning, in Genesis, it's about Adam and Eve enjoying walking with God in the cool of the day, in Revelation, the end, we will be with him, we will be in his presence for ever. To know his presence, to be in his presence is to encounter a love so deep and a life so rich that we will find ourselves longing to dwell with him, in his presence forever.

I love Psalm 84, which says this:

How lovely is your dwelling place,
  LORD Almighty!
My soul yearns, even faints,
  for the courts of the LORD;
my heart and my flesh cry out
  for the living God.
PSALM 84:1-2

We were made to know the presence of God. We were made to be home. For me, home and the presence of God are inseparable.

---

practise

Think for a moment about your own story, your own journey to faith. How did you first encounter God? Do you remember how things changed? How it felt?

- What single word would you use to describe it – was it a feeling of coming home, perhaps a feeling of being clean, quiet, perhaps a feeling of being accepted?

- When you encounter God's presence today, how does it feel?

- Spend some time thanking God for his presence today.

closer than a brother

'Here I am! I stand at the door and knock. If anyone hears my voice and opens the door, I will come in and eat with that person, and they with me.'

REVELATION 3:20

I was sixteen, I'd done Alpha, I'd been filled with the Holy Spirit, and a few months after that, I was at church. There was an American pastor called Brent Rue speaking at the service, and he started talking about a relationship he was in. He was saying,

> *'We get up in the morning and we go for a run, we get home and we'll have a coffee, and we'll read the paper together, and then we'll get ready for work and go to work together. Often during the day if there's something I'm not sure about, we'll talk about it.'*

I was thinking, 'Wow, this is a really extraordinary relationship, I don't know many people who do everything with a spouse or a friend.' And the more he said, the more extraordinary it sounded. I'm not always that quick to pick things up, and it took me a while to work out he wasn't talking about his spouse, or his roommate. He was talking about his relationship with Jesus!

The more he talked, the more gripped by what he said I became. It was utterly compelling. The way that he spoke about having a relationship, a deep friendship with Jesus, was so unlike anything I had ever heard before. As he talked, I found myself more and more desperate to have that kind of friendship with Jesus.

That talk, over thirty years ago, has probably informed more of my life of faith than any other talk I've heard. I've spent the time since then chasing after, and longing for, and aspiring to have that kind of friendship with God.

A great longing of my heart is to be a friend of God. My intention and hope for you as you read this book is that what I write stirs a longing within you and me to encounter friendship with God on an ever-deepening level.

I want to recommend a book to you; it's by Brennan Manning, and it's called *The Furious Longing of God**. It's a brilliant book about the love of God, friendship with God, and I try to read it every year. Every time I read it, I find myself drawn again, to know, to walk with, and to enjoy being with the one whose love for us is more abundant and extravagant than we will ever know.

MORE THAN A FEELING

We live in a culture that is very feelings-driven – in relationships, particularly romantic ones, often people will say, 'If I can't feel it, it's not real'. It's worth reminding ourselves that intimacy is not necessarily a feeling. True intimacy is, in my experience, often about so much more than what we might be feeling.

I support Fulham football club, which has been something of a journey of faith over the last few seasons! Sometimes I feel passionate about being a Fulham fan, other times I kind of forget about it. It's not that I don't support Fulham anymore, it's just that I'm not feeling massive enthusiasm; particularly when we get beaten by a League 1 team, as we did a while back! How I feel about Fulham may change, but my support for them doesn't.

The reason we talk about the presence of God before we talk about intimacy with God is that you can't experience intimacy with someone you don't know is there, someone you have not learned to be present with. Intimacy is something that grows. Feelings may

---

* Brennan Manning, *The Furious Longing of God* (David C. Cook, 2009)

play a part, but we should not base our whole faith experience on what we're feeling.

I may wake up tomorrow morning not feeling particularly close to Jesus. It may be because I didn't sleep well, it may be because although I was supposed to eat supper before I went out last night, I ran out of time so it was sitting in the warming drawer at home waiting, so it was dry by the time I got home, and I've eaten late so I don't sleep that well ... and I wake feeling a bit weary. Or I may wake up worrying about something, I may wake up excited about something, but I may not wake up feeling the presence of God. The important thing to remember is that it has nothing to do with how much he loves me, how much he loves you, or his presence with me, because he's promised both: he's promised that he loves me and he's promised that he is with us, regardless and sometimes in spite of how we feel.

What I'm learning is that intimacy is often as much about a choice as it is a feeling. Maturity in faith is choosing to pursue intimacy whether I feel God's love in that moment, or not. It's about activating choice and activating a decision in me, regardless of what I feel. It's worth remembering that God's love for each one of us is as unceasing as it is relentless – that is what he promises. He doesn't love us in response to our love for him, he loves us because he loves us, because we are his children.

He says that we are the apple of his eye, that he has written our names on the palms of his hands, and he's promised that he rejoices over each one of us with singing. He says that he's loved us with an everlasting love, and with loving kindness he has drawn us. Or, as Eugene Peterson puts it in *The Message* translation of Jeremiah 31:3, 'I've never quit loving you, and never will. Expect love, love, and more love!'*

We'll only really ever begin to understand intimacy with God, and know intimacy with God, when we begin with his love.

There will be times when we experience and encounter this as a feeling, as an emotion, but there'll be times when we don't. That is okay!

---

* Psalm 17:8; Isaiah 49:16; Zephaniah 3:17; Jeremiah 31:3, MSG.

In times when perhaps we aren't feeling close to him, or experiencing his love for us, we need to remember that his love is extravagant; it's written all over the pages of the Bible. We're hardwired to know that love, and to walk closely with him, to be his friends.

HE INVITES US TO BE HIS FRIENDS

The whole narrative of the Bible reminds us over and over again that he invites us to walk in increasingly intimate relationship with him. We're reminded of that in Genesis, where we are shown this beautiful picture of what intimacy with him looks like, with Adam and Eve walking with God in the cool of the day. Then again, right at the end of the Bible, in Revelation, Jesus says:

> 'Here I am! I stand at the door and knock. If anyone hears my voice and opens the door I will come in and eat with that person, and they with me.'
>
> REVELATION 3:20

Notice that Jesus says if *anyone*. His invitation is not just to those with saint-like holiness, or the hyper-religious, or the super-spiritual, or those who do amazing things for God; he says, 'If *anyone* hears my voice.'

That is a huge relief! Anyone can hear his voice and open the door. We are not qualified by what we've done or disqualified by what we have or haven't done; we are included in this invitation because of his love of us, and what he accomplished for us on the cross. The cross is the gateway to friendship and intimacy with God. He offers us an invitation that if we seek him, we will find him, that he will come and he will meet with us. James writes, 'Come near to God and he will come near to you.'* What a promise!

HE ALLOWS US TO GET TO KNOW HIM

One of my favourite verses in the Bible is 'My sheep recognise my voice. I know them and they follow me.'** Friends know what each

---

* Jeremiah 29:13; Psalm 59:10; James 4:8.
** John 10:27, MSG.

other's voices sound like, even in a room full of people. Our friend Katie has one of the most infectious laughs I know. Nici and I can tell if she is in a room while we are still walking towards it if she is in there laughing.

Jesus reveals his true nature, his very heart to his friends. I love the way that Jesus went out of his way, particularly to his three closest friends, Peter, James and John, to reveal who he was. He takes them up a mountain and is transfigured in front of them; in that moment they are allowed to see behind the curtain, so to speak, a glimpse of who he really is. Even then, they have to be reminded to listen – Peter is still talking, when a voice from the cloud says, in effect, this is Jesus, this is who he really is, pay attention: 'This is my Son, whom I love; with him I am well pleased.' In his darkest moment in Gethsemane, on the night that he knows he will be betrayed by a friend, arrested, tried and ultimately executed, it's those same three people he wants to be with him, to share his most vulnerable and anguish-filled moments with.*

He has other remarkable relationships. I love the friendship that he has with Mary and Martha; they seem to have this very real and honest relationship with him. In Luke's Gospel, we see how he loved how Mary sat listening to him when Martha was busy being busy around the house, and there's this glorious almost passive-aggressive moment when Martha, who's been tidying up, turns to Jesus and says, 'Lord, don't you care that my sister has left me to do the work by myself?' and Jesus doesn't rise to it; he says, 'Mary has chosen what is better.'**

When Martha and Mary's brother Lazarus dies, they're not afraid to tell Jesus, in no uncertain terms, what they actually think.*** That is what intimacy is; intimacy is about self-disclosure, it's about saying 'This is who I am – will you love me?' or 'This is who you are – I love

---

* Matthew 3:17; 26:37.
** Luke 10:38–42.
*** John 11:1–44.

you.' They know Jesus is a rabbi, but they also know him as a friend. What I've come to understand is that Jesus wants to share his heart, and everything that is most important to him, with his friends.

> *'I no longer call you servants, because a servant does not know his master's business. Instead, I have called you friends, for everything that I learned from my Father I have made known to you.'*
> JOHN 15:15

He says you're not slaves anymore; a slave doesn't have a conversation with their master, a slave does what they are told to do. He says you are no longer a slave, forced to live in performance mode, anymore; you do not have to earn anything. This relationship I've invited you to share with me isn't a meritocracy. I love you because I love you, because I love you. I want to relate to you as a friend. God promises:

> *'Call to me and I will answer you and tell you great and unsearchable things you do not know.'*
> JEREMIAH 33:3

Come to me.
Come.
It's an invitation, always, to come. Because he loves us.

HE CALLS US BY NAME

The Lord loves it when we make time to be with him. As we've seen, it's in his nature to reveal himself to his friends. And because of that, it is always personal. When he calls his friends, he calls us by name. Whether it's 'Moses, Moses'; whether it's 'Samuel, Samuel'; or whether it's 'Saul, Saul' he calls us by name. It's always personal.*

He talks to us by name.

---

* James 4:8; Exodus 3:4; 1 Samuel 3:10; Acts 9:4.

HE DRAWS US INTO CONVERSATION

The Lord wants to engage us in conversation. In Jeremiah 1:11 he says, 'What do you see, Jeremiah?' The reality is, he knows what Jeremiah sees in that moment, because he put that thought in Jeremiah's mind in the first place. The point is that what he is wanting to do in that moment is to invite Jeremiah to engage in a conversation with him.

God is always looking to get our attention and to draw us into conversation with him. Often, we want to *tell* God things, and he wants to talk *with* us. I'm often telling God things, putting the world to rights, and actually he just wants to talk. Asking God to tell us things can often be transactional. Engaging with him in a conversation is by nature relational. Other times, we want him to give us direction and he wants to talk to us about destiny: 'Lord, what should I do? Should I do this or should I do that?' and his response is, *'I love you. This is how I see you, and what I have for your life.'*

It's right that we talk to God about the big things that are going on in our lives. It's really important to do that, and to talk honestly and candidly about those things, knowing that he already knows and that he loves us. This should make us feel incredibly secure and enable us to be even more vulnerable with him.

With any friendship we also talk about the little stuff. It's important to talk about the little things, because the little things are often as important as the big things. Often, I'm learning, in friendships the big moments come about because of all sorts of little moments and conversations. That's what really deep friendships are about: life, death, the universe and everything in between.

My closest friend is called Piers, and I've known him since I was ten years old. Sometimes when we meet together, we talk about weighty matters of state, and we put the world to rights, or we'll talk about the things that are really important to us; other times, and these are sometimes the best times, we talk about totally random stuff. I'll get home and Nici will ask me what we talked about, and I'll say, 'I can't remember … but it was just really great to see him.'

I knew someone once, and every time I saw him all he wanted to do was talk about serious matters, and any conversation was intense and heavy. And that was fine, now and then, but after a while it was just exhausting!

In his book *Dirty Glory*, my friend Pete Greig says this, which I love:

> Your relationship with God is at its best when you talk to him about trivia ... I would hate it if my children only talked to me about Grave Matters of Serious Concern.*

As I said, we as a family are Fulham football supporters, and it has been an interesting couple of seasons, a rollercoaster for our faith. I sometimes pray for Fulham, but our boys have told me that I'm not allowed to listen to the match, because when I listen to it, we lose. (I think a little bit of superstition has dropped in there somewhere!) But anyway, we pray. For Fulham. And the prayers are sort of ... working. *ish*. I remember praying, 'Lord, it's really important that we win this match,' and then a thought came back to me which was, '*A lot of Luton fans are asking me the same thing for their team.*'

A few years ago, we were lucky enough to be season ticket holders and it would be fair to say that the season had been something of a disaster for Fulham. The first time we took the boys to a football match, when they were just old enough, on the way I said to them, 'Boys, you're going to hear all sorts of words that you've never heard before; please don't repeat any of them, but do ask us what they mean.' The result of that was that on the way home, little Jonah, who at that time was eight, turned and said to me, 'Dad, what's a ___?' – which I'll leave to your imagination, but it was what the guy sitting behind us had been calling the referee all match ... and he wasn't very happy with the referee!

---

* Pete Greig, *Dirty Glory* (Hodder & Stoughton, 2016) p79–80.

We were at a match in the middle of November – it was really cold and so we were all dressed up in our Fulham scarves, hats and gloves; you can imagine the scene – and the match wasn't going well. At all. We'd spent the entire game in our own half; in fact we'd spent the entire game defending our own goal – so basically in and around our own penalty box.

There was a man being particularly vocal behind us, who one of our sons had learned a few 'new words' from. He was getting more and more irate as the game went on, pretty much winding himself into a frenzy of sorts. And then, out of nowhere, I just began to become aware of the presence of God; it was sort of a mixture of just knowing and a sense of 'I think God is here.'

I didn't know God went to football matches, and so I said, 'Okay, God,' and the more I allowed myself to become aware of him, the more present he seemed to become; and that's often how it is. It's a bit like focussing your binoculars; you know there's something out there, and as you fiddle with the dial it begins to come more sharply into focus. It's often like that with the presence of God; if you just begin to become aware of him, if you push into that, you become more aware of his presence, and, if you don't, you become less aware of it. Sometimes I think the presence of God is like a butterfly looking for somewhere to land; and what I mean by that is he is always looking to make himself known, but it is so easy to miss, because it's such a light touch – it's not a heavy or intense thing.

So, there I am, with our boys, at a football match on a cold November evening, kitted out in Fulham Football Club apparel with a man behind shouting profanities at pretty much anyone other than a Fulham player or fan, I've become aware of the presence of God and I'm trying to work out what it all means, so I say, 'Okay, Lord, why are you here?' And he said, '*I like football,*' which I thought was fair enough. And then I said, 'What's happening?' and this thought comes into my mind:

> '*In a minute or so, the ball is going to be deflected, and it's going to get to this player on the halfway line; he's going to get the ball, he's going to run down the length of the opposition half and he's going to score a goal.*'

My first response is, 'That is a very random thought'. Often, I think that the more random the thought is, the more likely it's God (although I am by nature quite random – and I'm learning to discern the difference!). And so, I turn to our sons, and I say, 'In a minute, the ball is going to get deflected, and it's going to get to this player on the halfway line; he's going to get the ball, he's going to run down the length of the opposition half and he's going to score a goal.' And the swearing guy behind us happened to hear this, and he goes, 'Oh yeah, you'll be lucky mate!' (with a few extra new words for my boys to unlearn thrown in). Just as the words had left his mouth, the ball gets deflected, the player gets the ball, runs down the opposition half, and scores the goal. At which point the man exclaimed, and I won't repeat the words he used, but there were even more for our sons to unlearn, turned to me with his eyes wide and said, 'How'd you know that?' and I said … 'Oh, erm, I know the head coach,' and winked at our boys.

---

practise

God is speaking all the time. Remember Revelation 3:20: 'If anyone *hears* my voice.' The question is, have we intentionally turned to listen for his voice; have we taught ourselves to become aware of when he is speaking, of wanting him to speak to us? When we decide to listen, to hear his voice more clearly, then we become aware of his presence.

Think again about the story of Mary and Martha. Martha was busy serving, distracted with many things, but Mary sat at the feet of Jesus, giving him her whole attention, even though there was work to be done. Life can get crazy busy for all of us, and sometimes we need to down tools and focus on him and sit at his feet like Mary did. Sometimes we need to just stop. Put everything aside. And give Jesus our attention, whole and undivided.

Imagine that you are standing in a doorway. Jesus is standing at the front of the room, and you're about to walk through the door into the room, and he is there, waiting for you.

Whatever has happened today, in your day, good, bad or indifferent, imagine that your day is a suitcase, and just leave it at the door. Picture yourself putting it down and leaving it there, whatever it is – maybe it's a worry, maybe it's a health concern, maybe it's a conversation that you've had – but just picture leaving it at the door as you walk into the room. And then take a deep breath in, and a deep breath out. Do that a couple of times. And as you do that, I want you to imagine Jesus walking towards you.

What is the expression on his face?

What are you thinking, and seeing, and hearing, and feeling, in this moment, as he walks towards you?

As you reflect on these things, I want you to imagine that when he sees you, he smiles. And he does not stop smiling, until he is standing right in front of you. Then he reaches out and puts a hand on the side of your shoulder, and he begins to speak to you – not lots of words, but just one sentence. What one sentence, or one thing, is he saying to you?

What if he is saying, 'I am glad you're here. I've been waiting for you'?

I believe that is what Jesus would say, every time we begin to approach him. Just as in the parable of the prodigal son, when the father runs to meet his son, the Lord is the one who moves towards us. As soon as we start to move towards him, he moves towards us just as quickly, if not more quickly, because he's been waiting for us. Draw near to God, and he will draw near to you.*

I recognise that for some of us the very idea of intimacy with God might be a totally new idea. Perhaps, like me, your experience of church means that the very thought of friendship with God isn't

---

* James 4:8.

something you have ever even considered. It might also be that if you were brought up in a church tradition that particularly emphasised the holiness and majesty of God, the idea of intimacy with him feels foreign and perhaps slightly uncomfortable and overfamiliar.

My own experience is like that – if I did think about God, it was more of a distant holy God from school chapel or church growing up, who we should respect and revere – more as an idea than anything else, even if we didn't actually believe in him.

I am learning that actually it's not an either/or – God as my best friend or God as holy and living 'in unapproachable light'* – actually he is far, far more than that. He is both. He is more glorious, more holy, more awesome, more powerful than we can imagine, but he is also the one who loves us, who runs to us, who wraps his arms around us, who welcomes us home and throws a banquet for us because we have come safely home. He is the one who invites us to be his friends.

Fundamentally, what we believe about who God is, and what we believe about how God thinks about us, shapes how we approach him. In the last thirty years, the more that I have tried to read the Bible, and the more that I have tried to pray and spend time in, and enjoy his presence, the more I have come to encounter a God who is both my Father and my friend and like Aslan in CS Lewis' Narnia books – powerful and tender.

Intimacy with God, or indeed anyone else, takes time and it takes courage to be vulnerable. It takes time for us to grow in friendship and it takes courage to come to him as we are, warts and all, and say 'This is who I am.' As we do, if we listen, we will hear him whisper gently, 'I have loved you with an everlasting love. And you are my friend.'**

---

* 1 Timothy 6:16.
** Jeremiah 31:3; John 15:15.

how wide and long, how high and deep

Follow the way of love and eagerly desire gifts of the Spirit, especially prophecy. For ... the one who prophesies speaks to people for their strengthening, encouraging and comfort.

1 CORINTHIANS 14:1-3

I remember seeing Richard standing at the back of the church. He was standing so close to the door that at any moment he could just slip out into the summer evening if he wanted to.

As I said, I have always felt drawn to those who seem disengaged, who would quite obviously rather be somewhere, anywhere else than in church and I have done ever since I became a church leader. I immediately feel an empathy for them, a compassion and a longing for them to experience God's love for them. Perhaps it's because they remind me of the part of my story where I had to go to school chapel even though I had no interest at all in being there and the whole thing seemed like a waste of time.

In this particular case I was also reminded, so clearly, of encountering the presence of God for the first time and the way that it had changed everything for me. In that moment, like so many other times before and since, I began to ask God, 'What is your heart for him? What do you have for him?'

As I prayed and looked at him, two things began to happen. The first was that I began to feel God's love for him. For me, in those moments it is as if that wonderful passage in Ephesians 3:14–19 comes alive and is activated within me. I am given a small window into 'how wide and long and high and deep'* his extraordinary love for that person is, and I pray for that person to know that reality.

The second thing that happened was that I saw a picture in my mind's eye of him at a very expensive tailor's being fitted for a bespoke suit.

As I saw this unfold in my mind's eye, I asked, 'Lord, what does that mean?' As I continued to pray, I began to understand that God was saying that there was nothing about this person that was the same as anybody else, ever, that he was totally unique. It was as if God was reminding me that he did not have a cookie-cutter personality. God had a tailor-made life for him. One that would fit perfectly.

Having received this insight I asked God, 'Is this something for just me to know so that I can add him to my prayer list, or is this something I should share with him?'

This is important, and we will talk more about it in Chapter 6, but the reason I do this is because I am learning that sometimes, if not *most* of the time, in these moments God is simply sharing his heart with me for someone, in much the same way as I might tell you how much I like someone we both know. It isn't something to be shared with anyone else – he is just giving me an insight into how much he loves someone.

On other occasions as I pray, I sense God telling me that this is something he would like me to share. As soon as I asked the question, I instinctively *knew* that this was something I should share with Richard, so I went up to him and said, 'We don't know each other very well, but you caught my eye during the service, and I've

---

* Ephesians 3:18.

been praying for you. I think that God may have shared something with me for you. Would you like to hear it? No pressure at all if you'd rather not. I would totally understand.'

He looked at me briefly and then said, 'Sure, why not?'

As I shared the picture that I had received, his whole countenance changed, his guard came down, his body language shifted, and he became really engaged in what I was saying. When I offered to pray for him, he replied without hesitation, 'That would be great!' When I had finished praying a short prayer, he said thank you and slipped out the door.

A year later I was standing outside the church door welcoming people as they arrived, and a man came and asked if I remembered him. I paused for a second or two – he looked familiar, but I meet so many people it is sometimes hard to put names and places to all the faces.

'A year ago, you came up to me at the back of church and said that you'd been praying for me during the service and that you'd thought God might have told you something for me,' he said, 'and you said as you'd prayed that you'd seen me at a tailor's, being fitted for a suit.'

Then I remembered.

'I just wanted to say thank you,' he continued. 'My friends had taken me to church a few times, and I went, even though it didn't do anything for me at all. Just over a year ago my friends invited me again, and I said I would come one last time, but that was it. And I guess as we arrived at church, I'd kind of dared God – I said "If you are real you need to prove it to me tonight. I want you to say something to that bloke Bill about me." As the service went on, I thought, "Phew, I'm off the hook," and then you came up and said what you did. What you said that evening changed my life.'

I've often reflected on that evening and what I said and did. What I shared wasn't, on the face of it, particularly profound. It was a picture of someone being fitted with a suit, and an encouragement that he was unique, and that God had a bespoke plan for his life. And yet something happened that night that had a life-changing effect on him. The reason it had the impact that it did, was, I believe, because it led him into an encounter with the One who knew him and loved him. And that is really what the purpose of prophecy is. To share the heart of God for someone in such a way that it leads to an encounter with Jesus.

The purpose of prophecy is to share the heart of God for someone, or for a group of people, with them in such a way that it leads to an encounter with Jesus.

That encounter may not happen there and then in that moment, but it will; at some point, something will be awakened in them by what you said. It may be when they go home; it may be when they process it with a friend that they will begin, or continue, to encounter Jesus.

THE KEY IS LOVE

I have a confession to make. I've been reading the Bible for thirty years and I've only recently made a connection between what Paul has written in 1 Corinthians 12 and 1 Corinthians 14. Which is, of course, 1 Corinthians 13.

At one level, I have known that 1 Corinthians 12, which is all about spiritual gifts and unity, is followed by a chapter all about love, and then culminates with Paul exhorting the Corinthian church to 'Follow the way of love and eagerly desire gifts of the Spirit, especially prophecy.'* But what I hadn't fully appreciated was both the power and importance of this.

We, or at least I, tend to read the Bible in segments – mostly in chapters. This isn't of course how Paul wrote his letters or how he intended them to be read. Most books, certainly the letters and gospels, were written to be read as a whole, in one sitting, and aloud to a group of people, and then passed on to another group. But when

* 1 Corinthians 14:1.

I read it, what it often looks like is this: I'll read the chapter about spiritual gifts. And then the next day I'll read those amazing and incredibly challenging words Paul writes about love in Chapter 13. And then perhaps a couple of days later I will pick up my Bible and read Paul's words at the beginning of 1 Corinthians 14 and not make the link, or not necessarily really let it take hold. I will not appreciate the connection and full meaning of what Paul is saying.

Having spent time explaining what the spiritual gifts are, why they are all so important and how they work together, Paul finishes what has come to be known as 1 Corinthians 12 by writing 'Now eagerly desire the greater gifts.' The problem is that this is often where we put our Bibles down. Or at least I did. But if we continued reading, he answers the question of 'How? How do we use spiritual gifts?' And he says,

'I will show you the most excellent way … '
1 CORINTHIANS 12:31

Paul uses the word 'love' nine times in thirteen verses. There is no other place in the Bible where love is used so many times.

'If I … do not … have love,' he writes, *'I gain nothing.'*
1 CORINTHIANS 13:3

The Greek word that Paul uses for love here is ἀγάπην. This is the love of God. It is love that is benevolent and unconditional. It was so contrary to the way that the Corinthian church thought, and perhaps the way we think, that Paul outlines what it looks like in practice:

Love is patient, love is kind. It does not envy, it does not boast, it is not proud. It does not dishonour others, it is not self-seeking, it is not easily angered, it keeps no record of wrongs. Love does not delight in evil but rejoices with the truth. It always protects, always trusts, always hopes, always perseveres.
1 CORINTHIANS 13:4–7

This is a radical love. A love that transforms. A love that, as Paul writes, '*Never fails.*'*

And this famous exposition on love is not part of a marriage sermon – it is given in the context of Paul's teaching on exercising spiritual gifts in the church. This is the prerequisite that Paul says we need to be operating out of when we exercise any spiritual gift. Love. This kind of love. It is a high standard. It is not about us, it is not about how well we move with a gift, it is about how we use it. And it must always be from a place of love. We can't love like this without God. Without him working in and at our hearts.

And then, in 1 Corinthians 14:1, it is as if Paul is saying, now that you are starting to get how important love is when using this gift – if you love someone, you will want to prophesy, because in your love for them, you will long for them to know this love which is revealed as we prophesy.

It is as simple as it is profound. Love is the key. It isn't about clever words, it isn't about how articulate we are, or our powers of persuasion. It is about love.

DRAW OUT THE GOLD

We often tend to see the worst in ourselves. We know our own deepest darkest secrets, and depending on where our self-esteem is at a particular time, we might like ourselves a little bit, a lot, or not very much at all. If you are anything like me, sometimes this can all be at the same time! We can tend to disqualify ourselves from all kinds of things because of this.

The amazing thing is that God does not see us that way; if we are Christians, he sees us through the lens of Jesus. In Colossians 3:3–4 Paul writes,

> *For you died, and your life is now hidden with Christ in God. When Christ, who is your life, appears, then you also will appear with him in glory.*

---

* 1 Corinthians 13:8.

You are hidden with Christ, so when God looks at you, he sees Jesus in you. He sees the best version of you. He sees the version of you and me that we long to be, on our best day, with the sun in our face and the wind behind us. That is the version of ourselves that God sees. And his longing is that we, or the person we are talking to, has that awakened in them so that that realignment begins or continues to happen.

We see this again and again in the Bible:

- In Judges 6:11–24, when the angel of the Lord appears to Gideon, he says, '*The* LORD *is with you, mighty warrior.*' You can almost imagine Gideon looking around wondering who he's talking to, but the angel of the Lord is essentially saying, 'This is who you are; that's how I see you. So, become who you already are.'
- In Matthew 16:17–19, Jesus changes Simon's name from Simon to Peter. Simon means broken, bruised or damaged reed. This is the name he has carried around with him all his life; something brittle, something potentially damaged, something that is not everything it could be. And Jesus says, 'You are no longer Simon, you're Peter, you're Rock. Become who you already are; step into who I already see you as being.'*

What the Lord is doing in those moments is that he is calling the future and the destiny that he has for that person into the present moment. He's saying become who you already are. Become the person that I have a destiny for.

Often our self-perception is misaligned – it does not square with God's perception of us. It may be because of things that people have said to us, or because of things that have happened and things we

---

* There are a number of other significant name changes in the Old Testament, which are worth exploring. For example, Abram (exalted father) became Abraham (father of a multitude), Sarai (my princess) became Sarah (princess), and Jacob (supplanter) became Israel (prevails with God).

have come to believe about ourselves, while God's perception of us may be diametrically opposite, as far as the east is from the west, or it may be somewhere in between.

Sometimes God allows us to see what he sees in a person. Or we might ask God to help us see the person in front of us as he does. And, when we've asked the Lord if what he shows us is to pray about or to share with the person, we may begin to share with them how God sees them, what his heart for them is. And that brings someone's self-perception in line with God's view of them. That is what prophecy is. When you're prophesying, you're saying, 'This is who you are; this is who God says you are.' Some people call this *drawing out the gold.*

DELIVER IT WELL

When we share a word with someone, we need to do it well.

To really activate a word for and in somebody, we need to engage their imagination, so tell them the picture and invite them into that picture by sharing it with them. If we take people through that process, it's amazing how they engage. It is saying, 'This is what it means; this is the difference.' This means that we have to really think through and rehearse in our minds what we are going to say to people.

Prophecy has in the past sometimes had a bit of a chequered history in the church. One of my friends who leads a church told me that it is the gift that the church most needs and it is also the one he was most worried about being used. When I asked him why, his answer was that all too often he had seen a well-meaning person share something that was in his words 'only half-baked.' What he meant by that was that it was often perhaps the beginning of a divine thought or idea but that it hadn't been processed properly – or at all – and was often something of a stream of consciousness that created more confusion than help.

As church leader myself I have some sympathy with this. Imagine what would happen if I arrived at church to speak and just said the first thing that came into my head; people, because they are kind, might humour me once or twice, but after that they might look at the speaking rota to see who was speaking before deciding whether to come or not …

The book of Isaiah isn't a stream of consciousness. It has been thought about, and wrestled through, and inspired. There's a big narrative going through it. If we want to get really good at this – and I don't know about you, but I want to get really good at this – then we have to do the hard work. This involves doing it in such a way that it becomes second nature. Nothing starts by being second nature; it starts with (in my case) making a complete mess of it, and being unconsciously incompetent, and then I begin to realise that I'm being unconsciously incompetent, and then I think about who I can put around me to get better at this, and then I begin to become consciously competent, and then, eventually, hopefully, one day, I will end up being unconsciously competent – but I'm not there yet.

When I speak, I have spent many hours thinking, reading, praying and preparing. If we want prophecy to be a part of our church experience, and to see it grow in the life of our church families, we need to take it as seriously as we do the rest of the service.

There are of course moments when things seem to happen in real time – when we are receiving and trying to interpret what God might be saying, and whether we should be sharing it, all at the same time. But even then perhaps we should spend a moment or two processing it before we commit to sharing it!

What I really want to encourage you to get better at is being ready to become aware of God's presence, and to hear him speak at any point and in any place, not just in church. To let that word marinate – give yourself time to think it through, process it, and then reflect on how, if you were on the receiving end of this word, it could be the most encouraging, most life-giving, most forward-propelling realigning word that you could get. That's what we want to do: to serve people, not with the crumbs, but with the best meal that we could possibly give them.

How might this work, and how might we articulate this outside a church context, in a world that is in desperate need of hope, but often suspicious of religion?

SEEING WHAT GOD SEES

Before I was a church leader, I taught humanities in secondary schools in and around London. Much like my job now, I had a real sense of vocation and calling and loved working with the young people in those schools.

I used to arrive at the school early and walk round my classroom asking God to help me be the best teacher I could be, to do all I could to help the pupils realise their potential, and to see what often they couldn't in themselves. For me that was as much about what happened outside the classroom as what happened when I was in the classroom.

As a teacher I was keenly aware of the position of trust and responsibility I had, and that while I would never hide my faith, it was certainly not my job to preach at the young people I taught. It was more a case of asking God to help my life to do the talking.

Any teacher will tell you that if not in every class, certainly in every year group, there are always pupils who, for many reasons, are challenging and disruptive. The reasons are often as complex as they are heartbreaking.

As I child I struggled to concentrate in class and was easily distracted. While I was never disruptive there were a couple of moments when I found myself in a fair amount of trouble. It might have been for that reason that I had a feeling of empathy for those pupils who found school a challenge and had become a challenge at school.

One of those boys at one of the schools I taught at was called Sam. Sam was a larger-than-life character who, as it turned out, for a number of reasons had a very sad home life. While his friends loved him, his teachers were often left exasperated by his defiance and refusal to do something sometimes simply for the sake of it, or to get a rise out of someone.

I remember watching him in the school lunch hall one autumn day creating chaos. As the situation unravelled, I began talking to God and telling him how sad the situation was. As I did, I started to feel an immense compassion for him, and it was as if I sensed God saying, *'One of the reasons you are here is for Sam. He has so much potential. It's just waiting to be unlocked. He's a leader. Show him how to lead.'*

As I watched one of my colleagues march him to the cool down room I said, 'Okay, Lord, but you are going to have to show me how. I have no idea what he needs or how to do it.'

I sensed a reply straight away, *'You need to see him the way I do. Then you will be able to tell him who he is.'*

I took a deep breath. 'Okay, Lord,' I said, 'but you are going to have to open my eyes!'

The more I thought about it in the following few days, the more I was drawn to the accounts of Jesus and those who everyone else had written off. One person in particular kept coming to mind: Zacchaeus the tax collector.

Here was someone who had become rich by overtaxing his own people. This would have made him a pariah and an outcast among them. It is telling that when he hears Jesus is coming through his neighbourhood, the only way he can see him is by climbing a tree. Perhaps if anyone else who was described as being small had wanted to get a glimpse people would have made space, but not Zacchaeus. He had ripped off and upset too many people.

You can imagine the crowd's surprise when Jesus stopped at the foot of the sycamore tree and told Zacchaeus to come down because he wanted to spend time with him. Surely not. Jesus must have got it wrong. Didn't he know what kind of man this was? But that was the point. Jesus knew exactly what kind of a man he was – and he saw something else. He saw the redeemed and transformed version of Zacchaeus. He saw the Zacchaeus that Zacchaeus longed to be, and by speaking to him and treating him accordingly, by saying in effect 'This is how I see you' and leading him into an encounter with the love of God, Zacchaeus began to become that person.*

It took a while, but over time I began in some small way to see Sam the way that God did. I began to feel my compassion for him, for his situation, grow. I found myself fighting his corner in the staff room when some of my colleagues were being less positive about him. I began to pray for him and, as I prayed, God began to speak to me about Sam again – how he saw him, what he loved about him, the future he had for him – not so much in terms of job trajectory, but more in terms of who he could become.

The following academic year I was given Sam's set to teach – it was a good reminder in some ways of what a challenge he could be at times. On the occasions when I found myself beginning to have the same attitude towards him as some of the other teaching staff, I'd ask, 'Help me to see him the way you do, Lord.'

Things began to change one lesson when Sam had been particularly challenging. By nature, I am a fairly patient person. It takes a lot for me to lose my temper, but this lesson it seemed like Sam had walked into the classroom looking for a battle, and then halfway through the lesson he began to be openly antagonistic.

'Lord,' I prayed silently, 'I am running out of ideas, patience and compassion. Please. I need your wisdom in this situation.'

Before I had even finished, what I can only describe as a knowing came into my mind. *'Tell him who he is.'*

'Sam,' I said. 'Can you just step outside the classroom with me for a moment.'

'Here we go,' he exclaimed with more than a hint of defiance. 'A shouting at, and then it's back to the exclusion room for me!'

---

* See Luke 19:1–10 for a full account.

As we stepped outside, he squared up to me as if I was about to unleash all my fury on him and said, 'Okay, Sir, go on then, hit me with it ... '

I paused. In that moment I began to become aware of the presence of God. As I did and moved towards it in my mind's eye, I felt a peace and a calm.

'Sam,' I said. 'You are better than this. You are more than this.'

He looked at me slightly confused. It was as if the wind had been taken out of his sails.

'Sam, when I look at you, what I see is someone with so much potential. You may not feel like it, but you are. I can see it even if you can't.'

Sam looked really confused. I could see him trying to work out what was going on. Whatever he thought was going to happen when we stepped out of the classroom into the corridor, it definitely wasn't this.

I looked him straight in the eye.

'More than that, you have thirty other pupils in that room who are all watching you, taking their lead from you. Imagine what could happen in that room with those thirty other pupils if you decided that you were going to give the lesson a go and try and lead by example. That would actually be the ultimate act of defiance. Imagine ... '

'Okay,' he murmured.

'If you do, I promise that I will do everything I can to help and support you. I will fight your corner for you. But it begins here, and it begins now, with you. Are you going to be who I think you are?'

There was a long silence. I could see him trying to make sense of what I had just said.

'Okay, Sir,' he said.

'Okay,' I replied.

Sam walked back into the classroom, sat down at his desk and looked at one of his friends who was looking at him, along with the rest of the class, a little confused.

I never had a problem with him after that. Occasionally he might be a little distracted or talkative, but it really was a turning point, in my lessons at least.

Over time, the conversation around Sam in the staff room began to change slowly. People commented that while he definitely had his moments, he seemed to have calmed down somewhat and was less disruptive.

During his final year at school, the school decided to start a pupil led school council. It was a way for the pupils to vote for a small number of their peers who would make up the school council and represent their views to the senior management team. It was a brilliant way of engaging the pupils with some of the decisions that were being made and that impacted them. As I thought about who I could encourage to stand for election, I was reminded of what I had sensed the Lord saying to me about Sam the previous year: 'He's a leader.'

I was aware that suggesting Sam run for election was a risk – not so much for him, but for me. I knew that while he had made some real improvements and had really started to turn a corner in terms of his behaviour, he was still a big character with previous form, and, given that, a pupil whose candidacy might not be entirely well received by some of my colleagues.

As it turned out, I had somewhat underestimated the strength of feeling my suggestion was met with.

'You are kidding?' One of my colleagues snorted when I told him that I was going to encourage him to stand for election. 'If he gets in it will make the whole thing a joke, and that will be on you, Bill.'

Many of my colleagues, it seemed, had long memories and were unwilling to entertain the idea that not only had he begun to change, but that also he might have something to add should he be elected.

I still remember clearly one of the deputy headteachers sidling up to me just before a staff meeting. 'High-risk strategy, Bill,' he said shaking his head. 'Very high-risk strategy.'

When the hustings came round, Sam did a really good job of saying why he thought he would be a good member of the school council. Watching him speak it was clear, given the right support and guidelines, he was a very good communicator. To his credit, as he spoke he acknowledged that his past misdemeanours, as he put them, may not make him the most popular choice with some of the teachers, but that actually he could represent the pupils who found school more of a challenge.

Sam got the single largest number of pupil votes by a considerable margin.

I haven't seen him for many years, but I still remember the last thing he said when he came to find me on his final day at school.

'Thanks, Cahusac. What you said that time in the corridor that day, and the way you stood up for me when I ran for council meant a lot.'

While I recognise that not every situation or challenging individual has a story like Sam's, it remains a powerful example of what can happen in someone's life if we begin to ask God to change our hearts and open our eyes.

There is gold to be found, even in the most unlikely people, if only we will ask God to open our eyes so that we can see it. We may have to allow that insight, that word, to develop and marinate over time, so that we are fully ready to deliver it well. We need to be ready to share this gold, the heart of the Father, in the hope and expectation that it leads them into an encounter with Jesus, whether they recognise him or not.

And then watch as they begin to become the person who God says they already are.

practise

○ Read 1 Corinthians 12, 13 and 14 aloud, in one sitting.

○ Reflect. What stands out to you as you read? What have you learned? About the gifts of the spirit? About the gift of tongues? About prophecy?

○ As you go through your day, whoever you meet with, connect with on email, message or phone, whoever simply comes into your mind, ask the Lord to enable you to see them as he sees them. Pray for them to know Ephesians 3:14–19, 'how wide and long and high and deep' the Lord's love is for them.

be ready

'My sheep listen to my voice; I know them, and they follow me.'

JOHN 10:27

I had completely forgotten about the whole thing until I got to the corner of the street. And just as I arrived, there she was, walking towards me, in her mackintosh, pushing a shopping trolley, exactly as I had seen her a few hours before, wearing that same coat, pushing that same trolley.

Let me take you back a few hours, a few days …

Jackie Pullinger, a missionary who has done incredible work with drug addicts and triad gang members in Hong Kong, had come to lead a short mission in our North London parish. Jackie could perhaps be described as combining the compassion of Mother Teresa with the directness of Margaret Thatcher, and is perhaps one of the most extraordinary people I have ever met.

At our first team meeting she went around the table asking everyone what word God had given to them for the meeting. As she got steadily closer, I could feel myself – and the other junior clergyman next to me – getting increasingly nervous. We hadn't come to the meeting with a word of any kind, far less one to share with the team. When it finally came to my turn, she looked at me and my fellow curate for a moment, and we hardly dared to breathe.

'You two are off the hook today, but tomorrow, I expect you to come with something God has said to you!'

I was terrified. But inspired.

'We expect God to speak to us,' Kai Son, a member of her team, himself a former heroin addict and triad member, explained to me afterwards. 'And because we expect him to speak to us, we are ready when he does. It's that simple.'

The following morning, I sought God, asking and expecting him to speak, and arrived at the meeting armed with a word and ready to give it. Kai Son was right; when we expect God to speak to us, we are ready when he does.

MEETING ROSE

And so, I had been diligently trying to put that into practice for the prayer meetings we held every morning of the outreach programme before going out onto the streets. One morning, as we prayed, I had seen in my mind's eye a picture, in the form of a moving image, of an elderly lady wearing a mackintosh pushing her shopping trolley towards the corner of the main walkway on the large council estate in our parish, which was just opposite our church.

As we spent time that afternoon on the streets, reaching out to the community, I threw myself into the work, enjoying meeting people, hearing their stories and talking with them. So much so that, not only had I lost track of the time, which for me was not unusual, but I had also totally forgotten the picture I had seen as we had prayed earlier in the day. I had also rather written it off as another example of my very random thoughts. 'It was probably nothing,' I decided.

And yet, just at the moment we got to the corner of the walkway, there she was, moving towards us exactly as I had seen her. It all came rushing back to me.

I would love to say that in that moment I knew exactly what to do, and guided by the Holy Spirit I approached her naturally and sensitively, and gently initiated a conversation.

If only.

'There you are!' I exclaimed, slightly wide-eyed, my mouth moving faster than my mind could possibly keep up, creating a moment which was later to be filed as yet another of those all-too-familiar 'What. Was. I. Thinking?' incidents.

'Er … ?'

'I had totally forgotten about you until we got here!'

This was going from bad to worse. My mind was desperately trying to catch up with my mouth, my heart was firmly ensconced in my mouth and beating double time, but somehow the words kept coming.

'This is so weird … I wasn't sure if it was me or God earlier.'

The elderly lady was now looking at me with a mixture of confusion and alarm.

'And to be honest, I didn't actually think he was speaking to me. I thought it was my imagination running ahead of me.'

She was most definitely looking at me with alarm now.

I don't know if you have ever had one of those moments where you feel like you are standing by watching the most surreal and awkward exchange occur, while aware that you are the person in the middle of the conversation who is making it surreal and awkward, and not having a clue how to either metaphorically pull the rip cord, slam on the emergency brakes or just be spontaneously transported from the whole situation that moment.

'Are you alright, Father?' the lady asked.

'Father?' I was the one who was confused now. 'Father?' I asked again, just so that she also knew I was confused. She pointed at my chest. It was then that I remembered. I was, on this rarest of occasions, wearing my clerical shirt and collar.

'Oh, yes! Father!' I exclaimed.

I was confused. She was confused. The situation was confused. At which point Kai Son arrived.

'Bill, is everything okay?' he asked.

I looked at the lady, who was still looking at me.

'Yes. Well, sort of. I was trying to explain to this lady … ' I murmured.

'Maybe you should start again, by introducing yourself,' encouraged Kai Son, 'and then explain what you are doing.'

I paused, took a breath and started again. 'I'm so sorry,' I said. 'My name is Bill, and I am one of the clergy from the church across the road.'

The lady looked somewhat relieved that Kai Son had arrived and offered some direction.

'We're doing a community outreach week as a way of building relationships and developing friendships with people in our parish,' I explained. 'It has been great to get to know some of our neighbours and see how we can work together to build a stronger sense of community,' I continued.

I was about to launch into an explanation of the picture I had had earlier in the day when I remembered what Kai Son had told me: 'You don't need to tell people how you got to the word or picture you received, or even everything that you received, just the bit that is pertinent for them. The bit that will matter to them.'

I paused again, trying to remember what I had earlier dismissed as my own thoughts and imagination, and to work out how to articulate what I had seen in a way that would be accessible to this lady. She had after all just been on her way to do her shopping, and had been ambushed by one of the local priests who she had never met before.

Kai Son's advice was ringing in my ears. 'Remember to keep it normal, Bill. Or at least as normal as you can make it. The supernatural is called the supernatural because it should be both super and also natural!'

I remembered that when we had been praying, after seeing the lady who I was now trying to have a conversation with, I had seen a rose.

The lady was still looking at me, waiting for me to say something.

'I don't suppose a rose means anything to you?' I asked tentatively.

She laughed. 'I should think it does,' she said in a broad Northern Irish accent, 'it's my name!'

'Rose?' I asked again, just checking I had heard her correctly.

'Yes?'

'That's your name?'

'Yes, it is,' she replied with a smile.

It was at this point in our interaction (which, although it felt like it had been an accident happening in slow motion, had actually only lasted a minute or two) that I began to feel a sharp pain in my right hand.

I remembered Kai Son saying that often it is as we step out in faith as naturally as we can and begin to see that God has been speaking to us that he will give us another bit of information that he wants us to share in the conversation we are having. 'This may come in any number of ways,' he said, 'so you need to begin to be aware of anything you see in your mind's eye, or discern or feel either emotionally, or as a physical sensation in your body that you did not have until that moment.'

'Rose, I hope you don't mind me asking, but do you ever get sharp pain in your right hand?'

She held out her right hand and tried to clench it for me.

'Arthritis, Father,' she replied. 'It's agony. I can't sleep some nights it is so painful.'

'Rose, I'm so sorry to hear that. It does sound really painful – do you need help with anything?'

'I don't need any practical help, Father, but if you could pray, that would be kind.'

She didn't want prayer there and then, but I assured her that I would pray. Just as we were parting company, she looked at me. 'Funny thing is, Father, I haven't darkened the doors of a church for years, but now that we've met, well, maybe I will.'

Rose and I became friends after that awkward introduction. We would chat when we saw each other out on the housing estate, or in the local shops. She did also often come, just after the start of our Sunday morning services, and she would sit quietly at the back of the church 'taking it all in,' as she put it.

I've thought about that initial meeting with Rose many times over the years, and a number of things have struck me, and stayed with me:

Who, me?

Looking back, it was fairly clear that, although I was trying to hear God for the prayer meeting that morning, I had little expectation that God would speak to me, and certainly not about someone outside the meeting, someone we would meet later that day. I believed that God *did* speak to people in this way, and had seen him do so on occasion. I believed that God *could* speak to me in this way. But I didn't think he *would*. Why would he? There were, after all, far more spiritual people than me around, with far more experience. And I, like so many of us, looked at my own spiritual life and found myself wanting, and disqualified myself on that basis. God, I thought, only spoke like that to people who had put in the hard hours, and had devotional miles on the clock, so to speak.

Is it just me?

Secondly, even when I had begun to faintly wonder if God might be saying something to me, I kept questioning whether it *was* actually him speaking. I suspected I was making it all up – out of a desire to grow in friendship with him and to get better at encountering his voice for other people.

These two thought processes are not uncommon. While they are both totally understandable, they both, in my view, are often born out of a lack of expectation. A lack of expectation that God would speak to us, and a lack of expectation that we might actually be able to recognise it when he does!

WHO, ME?

It's important to remember, and to remind ourselves that God *wants* to speak to us – it is in his nature. Jesus is described as 'the Word.' He is the one who 'calls his own sheep by name,' and goes on to say, 'My sheep listen to my voice; I know them, and they follow me.'*

God wants to speak to us, even if we might *feel* far away from him or insignificant. As my friend Giles once put it to me, 'Billy, if God spoke to a paranoid megalomaniac ruler like Nebuchadnezzar, who was on the face of it about as far away from the kind of spiritual giant we think God speaks to as one can get, he can, and probably is speaking to you!'**

IS IT JUST ME?

Perhaps the problem for some of us, certainly for me at least, is more to do with the *way* that I expected God to speak to me. If I always (or even sometimes) expect him to speak to me by writing with fire in the sky I may be setting myself up for disappointment.

But if I open my Bible knowing and reminding myself that it is the word of God, and expecting him to speak through it, then whenever I read it, he *will* be speaking to me – sometimes through a particular verse, and other times over a period of time as a theme, or themes, emerge. It is as we read his word and begin to see how he speaks to us through it, and about what, that we then begin to recognise other times and contexts when he might also be speaking to us. That, I think, is what Jesus means when he says his sheep listen to his voice; that they know and follow him.

* John 1:1; John 10:3, 27.
** You can read the story of Nebuchadnezzar in Daniel Chapters 2 and 3. It's worth remembering that God doesn't just speak to Christians, or people who know him; there's a very clear biblical precedent for this. Whether it is Pharaoh through his dreams in the story of Joseph, or Nebuchadnezzar in the book of Daniel – neither of whom, I think it's fair to say, would be considered to be believers in the God of the people of Israel – the Magi in the nativity narrative, Pontius Pilate's wife, or even, and perhaps most dramatically, to Saul as he travelled the road to Damascus to arrest followers of The Way.

I knew that in theory. There were times when I prayed, whether for myself or for someone else, and a Bible verse would come to mind. I just didn't expect God to do anything more than that, or I dismissed it as 'just me'.

When it comes to distinguishing between the voice of God and our own thoughts and imagination, there are some principles worth considering.

First is to ask three questions about any word we think God has given us:

○ Is it strengthening, comforting and encouraging?*
○ Does it reflect the nature of Jesus as revealed in the Bible?
○ Is it in accordance with biblical teaching and morality?

If the answer to any one of these is 'no' then, in my experience, it is unlikely to be from God – but if the answer to all three is 'yes', then it could well be. And although this might sound a complicated and somewhat contrived way of processing something that is at its heart relational, the more we can learn to think like this as we reflect on what we think God might be saying, the more natural it becomes – essentially, we move from conscious competence to unconscious competence.

Second is to think about where the thought came from. If it is unexpected, perhaps a totally surprising intrusion into a train of thought that has come from nowhere, that is sometimes a good indicator. We read in Isaiah:

'For my thoughts are not your thoughts,
    neither are your ways my ways,'
declares the LORD.
'As the heavens are higher than the earth,
    so are my ways higher than your ways
    and my thoughts than your thoughts.'
ISAIAH 55:8-9

* Hebrews 11:1.

God's thoughts are not our thoughts. A prophetic word, and hearing God's voice, is more than just a nicer version of a thought that we have had. We must avoid the trap of making God in our own image, whereby everything nice we think and everything we want to do is something we imagine God is saying, even giving us permission to do things that we wouldn't do otherwise. The prophetic is more than that. When God speaks, his thoughts are not our thoughts; sometimes they are in line with ours, or sometimes they're more amplified, and sometimes they are completely and utterly different.

CONFIDENCE

I have learned that when I'm made aware of an area of spiritual weakness, the best remedy is to recognise and acknowledge my own lack (in this case of expectation) and to take responsibility for my own growth – to read books, listen to podcasts and spend time with people who have more experience in the area, to put what I learn into practice and watch as, little by little, my own levels of expectation begin to increase.

With all these principles in mind, we can draw confidence, knowing 'faith is confidence in what we hope for and assurance about what we do not see,' and growing that faith and certainty comes from a hope built on the confidence that he has spoken to us before and that we have seen what can happen when he does.

The more we expect God to speak to us, the more we find that we do begin to encounter his voice. And the more we step out and share even something simple and obvious, and then see the impact that can have on the person we're sharing it with, the more our faith grows. Sometimes if we're prepared to go that little bit further than we think we have faith for, it's amazing how God will meet us.

Going back to my exchange with Rose, I had not expected God to speak to me, and when he did, I had not recognised it, assuming it was my own thoughts and imagination. As a result, I had absolutely no plan at all about how I might engage with Rose when I did meet her, and the encounter was like watching an accident happen in slow motion. Part of that was down to my inability in the moment to think on my feet and self-edit my externally processed thoughts, and part of it was because I was so surprised that God had actually spoken to me!

This is why it is so important to have thought through practically what a process might look like for engaging in a discussion, and also what to share and how to share it. We'll go into this in more detail in the chapters that follow. I encourage you to spend some time going through them, while also thinking of the one or two things you can apply straight away.

I would have had a much, much better initial interaction with Rose had I thought about what I had received when I received it, and then how to approach her when I saw her. It is actually very easy to open a discussion with anyone if we are self-aware and have a plan, even if it is a loose, vague one. We don't have to be an extreme extrovert, or a super-spiritual, faith-filled and gifted prophetic voice to do any of this – we just need to have thought it through ahead of time and have a love for people.

BE STILL, BE THANKFUL, BE PRESENT, BE READY

A few years ago, I was invited to speak at a conference in Spain. The church hosting the conference had kindly put me up in a hotel on the outskirts of town, and having arrived early, I decided to go for a walk along the river to stretch my legs and to think and pray through the next few days. I have learned that, given my temperament, if I pray sitting down, I often got distracted – or end up falling asleep. Also, my mind tends to work marginally better when I am moving, and I love walking, so I often go for a walk to pray.

As I walked, I took some time to ask the Lord if there was anyone at the conference that he might have a particular word of edification, strengthening or comfort for. Over the years I've developed a framework that helps me approach these times with expectation – *be still, be thankful, be present, be ready*.

Be Still

I started my time walking along the river by *being still*. While this sounds like a contradiction, I've learned that cultivating a posture and attitude of stillness is not necessarily about not moving; it is about stilling my mind and my heart – focussing on God and remembering who he is. I do this by slowly repeating 'I am my beloved's, and his desire is for me', while also focussing on my breathing. I breathe in slowly to the count of four seconds. I say (or think), 'I am my beloved's.' I then pause for a second, and then exhale to the count of four seconds speaking or thinking the second half of the verse, 'and his desire is for me.' The other verse that I often use is 'Be still and know that I am God,' this time breaking the sentence down into two four-word blocks: 'Be still … and know … that I … am God,' using the same four-second inhalation, a pause and then the four-second exhalation pattern.*

There are times when I spend a long time doing this, and others when I move through this part of my time relatively quickly. The length of time is less important than that my heart and mind come to a place where God is brought into focus, and nothing else – what has happened during the day, or the other things that can so easily distract. It is as I do this that I often become more consciously aware of God's presence – and as a result, of his love, his goodness, his holiness, his power.

* Song of Solomon 7:10, ESV; Psalm 46:10.

Be thankful

Once I begin to become aware of his presence, I spend time *thanking him* – for his presence, and for any number of other things, big or small. I may spend time thanking him for who he is, or for particular things that have happened. This isn't just a formula or a routine, it is about being proactive in reflecting what has been good, or what we have seen that is beautiful and thanking him for those things.

As I walked down the road, the sun was starting to go down and the sky was the most beautiful colour. 'Father, thank you that I am here with you and that I get to see this amazing sunset. Thank you that I got here safely. Thank you for the church's generosity. Thank you for everything you are going to do in these next few days,' I prayed.

Thanking God for what he is going to do is about creating an attitude of expectation in my own heart, remembering that he has promised that if we ask, we will receive, if we seek we will find, and if we knock the door will be opened to us, and that if we truly believe, we will receive whatever we ask for in prayer.*

Be present

It is at this point I begin to ask him if there are people who are going to be where I am that he particularly wants to reach out to and edify, strengthen and encourage – or all three. This is about *becoming present* to his voice as he speaks to us.

As I continued walking alongside the river, I had what I recognised was a knowing – a name began to come to mind, and the more I allowed it to settle, the more it seemed to come into focus – much like binoculars when we are focussing them. Initially I thought it was Daniel, but as I began to focus on the name, I sensed that it was Danielle.

---

* Matthew 7:7–8; 21:22.

'Father, thank you for Danielle. Thank you that you know her and love her, thank you that you want to speak to her.'

As I continued to be present to God and what he might want to say, I saw an image of her playing a flute in my mind's eye.

'Okay, Lord,' I prayed. 'Is there anything you want to say to Danielle who plays the flute?'

Immediately I felt a well of compassion surge within my heart, a tiny glimpse into the endless expanse of the heart of God.

'*I love her. I am with her.*'

'*I love her. I am with her.*'

Over and over again.

I had learned that while what seemed like obvious biblical truth is exactly that, it may not be as obvious to the recipient, and that just because it might seem obvious, my own insecurities about it being obvious and the temptation to want something more 'significant' needed to be recognised and moved beyond.

'Stick to what he tells you, nothing more, nothing less,' my friend Carl had told me once.

Be ready

At this point, I began to *get ready*. How did I frame what I had received for Danielle? What might be the best way to share it? How would I want to receive it if it was a word for me? How could I honour her in the moment?

Being ready means having prayerfully considered all of these things before I even meet Danielle. It means rehearsing in my own mind the words I might use so that what I believed God had said didn't get lost in a moment of flow of consciousness, making it up as I went along. There are times when we have to do this, and even in those I have learned to pause even a little bit so that my mind can keep up with what is happening, rather than racing ahead – the equivalent of the ten-second time delay that is sometimes deployed during live TV and radio broadcasts when they are not sure what might be said.

On this occasion I had the time to be still, be thankful, be present and be ready, and wanted to make sure I had made the most of that.

As the first session opened, after I had introduced myself to delegates in the auditorium, most of whom I couldn't actually see due to the lights which were so bright I couldn't see past the second row, I took a breath.

'I wondered if there is anybody here called Danielle?' I asked. I couldn't see if there was, so I also asked if the main lights could be turned up so that people could see each other.

Two ladies had their hands up.

'Wonderful to see you both – it's great that you are here! Does one of you play the flute?'

One lady kept her hand up, while the other one lowered hers.

'Thank so much for saying you are here,' I said to the Danielle who had lowered her hand, 'I would love to say hi at the end of the session, even though the word I believe I have is for the other one of you – is that okay?'

'Of course – thank you!' she said, smiling as she sat down.

'Danielle, you do play the flute, right?' I asked just to double-check.

'Yes, but not as well as I would like.'

I looked at her for a moment. 'Danielle, when I was praying earlier you came to my mind, even though we have never met before. God told me your name, and that you played the flute.'

I could feel the compassion rising within me again. 'Danielle, what I have for you is this – as I prayed God kept saying to me, "I love her, I am with her", over and over again. I don't know if that means anything to you or not, but I have asked some of the team to pray with you at the end of this session if you'd like that?'

I could tell from her response that what I had said resonated with her on some level. 'Please do come and say hi after the team have prayed with you if you'd like,' I said.

The interaction was simple, clear and lasted less than a minute.

From what I gathered the team prayed with her briefly and then she left quietly.

Eighteen months later I was at the same conference, and as I arrived at the venue the pastor of the church came to say hello with a lady.

'Bill, do you remember this lady?' he asked. 'It's Danielle.'

'Danielle!' I said, remembering the word I had shared the year before. 'How are you?'

Tears began falling down Danielle's cheeks and, as she spoke, her voice began to crack with emotion.

'Just before the conference I had not been feeling very well. I didn't think there was anything seriously wrong but I wanted to be safe, and had some tests.' She paused for a moment, collecting herself.

'A week after you shared that word with me, I was diagnosed with cancer. It was a very, very tough time, and I was very ill, but the words you shared, that God loved me and was with me have carried me. I remember when you shared it thinking how simple it was,' she paused. 'And yet, even when I was so ill and afraid, those words kept coming back to me, kept me going, even on the darkest of days, reminding me that God loved me and that he was with me, so thank you.'

When we pray with expectation, we pray knowing that God wants to speak to us, and that he is more able to speak to us than we are able to hear him. As we do, by being still, being thankful, being present and then getting ready, we will see him step into even the most challenging situations and speak hope, often, as was the case with Danielle, before she even knew that she needed it.

practise

The next time you go to church or to a prayer meeting or gathering, spend some time beforehand preparing your heart and asking God to give you a word or contribution to the meeting, or to an individual there, even if there is no opportunity to share it. Perhaps go for a walk or sit in a quiet room. Follow the practice of: *be still, be thankful, be present and be ready.* Could you make this a regular spiritual discipline?

rushing waters
how God speaks,
and how we hear

His feet were like bronze glowing in a furnace, and his voice was like the sound of rushing waters.

REVELATION 1:15

God is speaking in many different ways.

Not long after we moved to Surrey, I went on a walk, and I listened to a stream. I walked past a Romany community; across a field there was a stream, quite a wide stream with a wooden bridge reaching across it. I was thinking about the verse in Revelation describing God's voice as the sound of rushing waters. I stopped at the stream and listened, and suddenly I understood. I understood that it was not just one sound, it was not just 'the stream'. Although on the one hand the sound was collectively the stream, on the other, when I started to listen closely, the water was going over stones, round tree roots, and actually the stream was making a lot of different noises. It was like an orchestra playing a piece of music – all sorts of instruments playing together in unison to create a beautiful sound. In the same way the voice of the Lord is like many rushing waters; when the waters rush, although if you listen just briefly you hear one sound, when you really focus in, you can hear all sorts of different sounds. God speaks on many levels and on multiple frequencies all at the same time. Over time we will pick up on particular things, particular melodies, rhythms or beats, depending on what is happening in our life or what our heart is particularly attuned to.

I have gone on that walk almost every day since. The stream is my favourite part of my favourite walk.

HOW WE ENCOUNTER GOD'S PRESENCE

God is always speaking and like rushing waters he speaks in many different ways. In the chapters that follow we are going to explore some of the specific and different ways through which God 'speaks'. But there are also many different ways we perceive him speaking – there are different ways we can encounter the presence of God. And each one of us is 'wired' slightly differently, and we tend to encounter the presence of God slightly differently, and differently in different seasons. Think, for a moment, about how you last encountered the presence of God.

Perhaps it was during worship; your imagination was activated and you began to enter into the worship in a different way. Or perhaps as you listened to the Bible being read something just came alive in you, or as someone started speaking or reading the Scriptures, you found yourself imagining you were there; and you were encountering the presence of God. You might have experienced something physical – a warmth, perhaps in the same way that John Wesley felt his heart 'strangely warmed' and the disciples on the road to Emmaus felt their hearts burning within them,* or you might have felt your heart beating strongly, or a trembling in your hands or feet. You might have very strongly just *known* something, *felt* a sense of peace, or perhaps you *saw* a picture in your mind's eye. You might even have *heard* something. These are the most common ways we

* Luke 24:32.

experience the presence of God – there are others, and we are all a little different. I knew someone once who would smell smoke, and that was a clear signal to her that she was encountering the presence of God.

There is no one fixed way that we hear God – we encounter him in different ways to varying degrees at different times, but this is a helpful starting point.

- Some of us are *knowers*; there are moments when we just *know* that God is present with us; perhaps in a gathering or in church we suddenly just know and we have this conviction that God is with us. It's not an emotional response, it's not a feeling, it's not a sense and we don't see anything. It is a conviction – we just know that he is with us. Or it might be as we read the Bible, our minds are opened, and we have insight and understanding.
- Some of us are *feelers*; the way we encounter the presence of God is through our feelings. So, perhaps in church, depending on what's happening in worship or in the talk, we will just feel something change in the environment, in the atmosphere. We encounter the presence of God and respond by how we feel: we might feel an overwhelming sense of peace, we might feel moved, we might feel a strong compassion for someone. Or it might be physical – a particular sensation in our bodies. Feelers tend to have an emotional or physical response to being in the presence of God.
- Some of us are *see-ers*, and we might often tend to see a picture in our mind's eye, or have an open vision of something, seeing a picture as if with our human eyes, as if it is really there.
- Some of us are *hearers*, and might respond to sounds, such as a bell, or hear a voice in our head, or receive the interpretation of a tongue, or even the audible voice of God.

I am, by nature, a feeler who thinks. In other words, my initial response is to feel something and then work out what I think about what I am feeling. Often at some point during a conversation I will *feel* compassion and empathy for the person I am engaging with. Sometimes it is almost as if in that moment I experience a small part of God's love for them. That also means I am constantly aware that the person I am with is loved by God and, for me, that grounds it and gives it meaning.

Not everyone is a feeler. Some people by nature are thinkers first. They then work out what they feel about what they are thinking. Neither is better or more effective than the other, and of course the reality is that humans are more complicated and nuanced. For a knower, in moments like the one I had with John, they need to know and remember that God loves the person they are with and to treat them accordingly. And, whether you are more of a feeler or more of a thinker, as best you can, lead with questions – it gives the person an out, and gives you an out should you need it!

WHERE WE ENCOUNTER GOD'S PRESENCE

I have a friend who has one of the busiest and most intensely demanding jobs I can think of. He works very long hours. He is also one of the most joyful people I know. When I asked him what his secret was, he said, 'The presence of God. Always the presence of God. Even though my work is very demanding, I take time between meetings or calls and still myself – I'll close my eyes if I can, breathe in and out slowly, remember that God has promised that he is with me and thank him that he is there, regardless of how busy life gets.'

Just as God is speaking all the time, he is everywhere, even in the midst of a busy working day. But there are some places where we are more aware of him, more able to focus on him than others. Jesus said to go into your room and shut the door to pray, while he himself would go up on a mountain to pray.*

As well as *how* you encounter the presence of God, think about *where* you encounter him. Some people might primarily encounter

* Matthew 6:6; 14:23; Luke 6:12.

God at church, whether it's in the silence of an ancient chapel on a kneeler, or in a large, brightly lit auditorium during worship. For some it may be on your own at home; some may encounter God in nature, when out on a walk. Some may encounter God when they are with Christian friends, whether or not that is in church.

There are lots of places people might encounter the presence of God and, as before, it's not either/or. We all move in and out of seasons where we encounter God one way or in a particular place, and then suddenly, or gradually over time, we're in another season where we encounter him in different ways and different places. But there's a kind of dance between how God shows up and when and where, and with our intentionality and how he responds to our intention, our desire to meet with him.

I want to encourage you not to settle for where you have become familiar with encountering the presence of God, but be open to encountering him in inconvenient places, at inconvenient times, and watch what happens.

For a large part of my life since coming to faith, I mostly encountered – or was mostly aware of – the presence of God in church; at other times, I have had a corner or a chair where I would sit and pray in the mornings. For a while I kept an extra empty chair there, which reminded me of the presence of the Lord. Or I have prayed in the car and imagined the Lord beside me in the passenger seat. And there are times when an hour in the middle of the night in a 24-7 Prayer room has been the place where I have heard from God most clearly. Another thing I have tried in the past is to set the alarm on my phone to go off at regular intervals to remind me that God is present; his presence is with me, wherever I happen to be, and whether I feel it or not. That is his promise: 'I am with you.'*

But in the season that I'm in at the moment, I tend to walk, and I'm encountering him more in unexpected places, especially as I

* Matthew 28:20.

spend time with those who aren't people of faith, as you will see from some of the stories in this book.

That might not have been my experience a couple of years ago, but I'm finding that more and more I recognise God's presence in places I don't expect, and then I allow him to interrupt me. I'm learning to remind myself that the presence of God isn't confined to a church building or a church service and that he is active in places I wouldn't usually expect. I try to be on the lookout for those times, when God does seem to be present and at work.

When I recognise those moments, I am learning to 'press into' them. I start with thanking him for his presence, and then ask him what he is doing, and then maybe ask for his heart and perspective on the person or situation and take it from there. The best way to describe it is looking for life and then embracing it.

ALLOWING GOD TO INTERRUPT

I walk our dog Marley (who on occasion does behave somewhat like her namesake in the film *Marley and Me*) first thing in the morning, and our favourite route also goes past an old house tucked away behind some trees.

At first, the man who lives there came across as a little unfriendly. Sometimes I would smile and wave as I walked past, and I would occasionally get half a wave back. That changed one morning when the man waved, a proper wave, as I walked past. Then, as I was walking back and passed again a little while later, he was driving towards his gate, and he parked his car and came out to meet me.

He said hello, and asked who I was, and I said, 'It's alright. I'm Bill; I'm a vicar.' We ended up having an extraordinary conversation that lasted probably an hour outside this old house hidden behind some trees at the bottom of the Surrey hills.

Two things happened: first of all, as we talked, he started sharing his story, and some of the things that had happened to him – the smile as he talked of one of his children with pride, the tears as he spoke of his grief at the loss of a family member. And lots and lots of questions – the ruminations of a soul longing to be heard. As I said, I've never met him before, and here he was pouring his heart out to me, a complete stranger, which as a pastor I always think is the most incredible privilege.

The other thing that happened was that as I stood there with him, as the conversation unfolded, I began to become aware of the presence of God. I hadn't gone walking in the hope of meeting someone for a conversation, I was actually trying to get away by myself, without interruption, so that I could begin to think about what I was going to preach on later in the week.

Once I got over my initial surprise at the nature of the conversation, the questions that went through my mind and the prayer I prayed was, 'Lord, what are you doing; what's happening here? What do I need to be aware of; is there anything I need to discern?'

The questions he was asking came out of nowhere, with no context, other than what he had shared, and here he was opening up and asking big, life-the-universe-and-everything-in-between questions. As we talked, he started to weep and he said, 'I can't believe I'm standing here, talking to you, a complete stranger, and crying and telling you all this – but you just make me feel very *at home*.'

I have come to recognise that these things only happen when God is there, when he's doing something. He wants people to encounter his presence and to know his love for them.

The next question I ask is always, what do I do? So, it started with a *knowing*, rather than a feeling; and as I listened to him, and as we began to discuss his questions together, I began to *feel* a compassion for him that was not my own.

What I mean by that is I began, in a small way, to feel an emotion, an affection for him which I have come to recognise is the Father's heart, his love, for somebody. When this happens what I try to do, in the middle of a conversation as I'm listening, is to allow that to inform how I respond, how I listen, how I answer or don't. So, it was first a knowing, then it was a feeling, then a little bit of all of it together.

I wasn't walking around praying or listening to worship music; I was just on my walk, someone waves, and the presence of God becomes amplified, at least to me. So be encouraged to be ready for and seek the Lord wherever you think or feel he is doing something; which could be anywhere. Allow him to interrupt you.

To learn to recognise the presence of God, and to step into it, could be described as like learning to swim and then leaping into a swimming pool – with or without arm bands. It is a profoundly joyful, life-giving moment.

Here's to jumping in.

---

practise

Are there particular places you encounter God's presence? When you are next there, spend some time in prayer, and reflect.

○ What is it about this place that enables you to know his presence?

○ Is it the same every time, or is it different sometimes?

○ Why do you think this might be the case?

CHAPTER 6

God-breathed

how God speaks through scripture

All Scripture is God-breathed and is useful for teaching, rebuking, correcting and training in righteousness, so that the servant of God may be thoroughly equipped for every good work.

2 TIMOTHY 3:16–17

GOD SPEAKS THROUGH HIS WORD

I was having a long talk with my friend Giles. I must have been in my late teens and he was a few years older, and along with a few others had taken me under his wing when I first came to faith. No question was ever too stupid or irreverent. He had that rare mix of strength of character, directness and kindness that made him very approachable. He listened to me as I talked about wanting God to really speak to me and telling him about some of the ways I had seen and heard others encounter his voice. My great desire was to really know God, and to recognise when he was talking to me and what he was saying. After I'd finished, he paused for a moment. I'm sure he could hear my sense of frustration.

'Billy,' he said gently, 'when was the last time you think God spoke to you?'

'I'm not sure,' I replied, somewhat confused.

'Okay, let me ask you another question. When did you last read your Bible?' he asked with a smile.

'This morning,' I offered.

'And what do you remember about what you read?' Giles asked.

I paused. 'It was about Jesus calling Zacchaeus down from the tree and saying he wanted to spend time with him … and then Zacchaeus saying sorry for taking people's money and saying he would pay it back.'

'That's brilliant, Billy. What did you take from that?'

I thought for a moment. 'That Jesus saw Zacchaeus amidst the noise and the crowd, even as he was up a tree, and that no matter what he had done, Jesus still wanted to spend time with him. And that when Jesus saw him his life began to change.'

'And what does that tell you about Jesus?' asked Giles, leaning in.

I reflected on the question briefly. 'That Jesus sees people, even in a crowd, and that he wants to spend time with them regardless of their past mistakes or what they might have done.'

'Sounds to me like God spoke to you this morning,' said Giles, leaning back in his chair smiling. 'The rest, however amazing, is the icing on the cake, Billy, the icing on the cake. More than that, he will never say anything that is contrary to what is in the Bible. It is the gold standard.'

As the conversation went on Giles explained that the primary way that God speaks to us is through the Bible. For many people that may not be rocket science, but for me, as someone new to faith, this was perhaps one of the most important lessons I ever learned. If I wanted God to speak to me, the first place I needed to go was the Bible.

Looking back on that time, I think that two things were happening. The first was that I really wanted God to speak to me in a *particular way*. I had seen and heard amazing stories of God speaking powerfully to people in dreams, visions, audible voices or knowings, and I wanted a similar experience. I remember thinking that it must be a marker of the depth of that person's relationship with God when they had experiences like these. To be honest, I suspect that on an unconscious level I came to think that *how* God spoke was more important than *that* he spoke.

The second was that I was overthinking it. I'm learning that sometimes we can want something so much that we miss it because we are so focussed on the *how* that we miss the *who*. I have come to really appreciate the quote, 'Ask God to speak to you and then get on with your day.'

Over the years, since that discussion with Giles, I have had similar conversations with many people – people who longed to know God better and grow in their friendship with him, people who are either struggling to encounter God's voice at all, or who are finding it hard to discern what he might be saying to them – and I always ask the same questions he asked me.

The primary way God speaks to us is through the Bible. The Bible is the word of God; if we want to know what God thinks about all sorts of things, the best place to start is the Bible, and arguably the place to finish is the Bible.

As I have reflected on the central importance of the Bible, I have often been brought back to two scriptures. The first is John 10:27, 'My sheep listen to my voice; I know them, and they follow me.' The second is 2 Timothy 3:17, 'All Scripture is God-breathed and is useful for teaching, rebuking, correcting and training in righteousness, so that the servant of God may be thoroughly equipped for every good work.'

If we want to know God better, we need to listen to his voice – to read the Bible. That is how we get to know him. The better we know him, the more we begin to recognise when he is speaking, and what he might be saying. No matter what we might feel, or see, or hear or know, if it is genuinely God speaking to us, he will always be consistent and true to what he has revealed to us about himself, and what he thinks about things, in the Bible.

There are, of course, things that God does not address directly in the Bible, but while he may not have covered the issue head on, he will always have a principle that he has spoken about that we can go back to.

As I think back on times when I have prayed with people, I am also reminded that in a vast majority of cases, he has often brought a scripture to mind, and these have often been the things that have brought the most strengthening, comfort and encouragement* to the recipient.

THE WHOLE BIBLE

I make it my practice to try to read through the whole Bible every year. When someone first mentioned it to me, the thought of reading the whole Bible through seemed quite intimidating, but I found that having a guide to follow really did help. There are many different programmes available, and I've listed a few below, but one that I've been using recently is Nicky and Pippa Gumbel's *Bible in One Year*. That one is particularly helpful, as not only does it break the Bible down into manageable daily passages, but it also has a brilliant commentary and the option to read or listen to the audio version.

A Bible reading plan encourages you to read all of the Bible, rather than just the bits that you like. There are passages that I wouldn't read as often, or at all, otherwise. I remember one morning a number of years ago seeing that one of the daily passages from the *Bible in One Year* was 1 Chronicles 1. I let out a bit of a sigh – I knew the passage, it was the historical records from Adam to Abraham, a list of names. I was all set to just move on and ignore it when I sensed that gentle whisper in my inner ear: '*These names are here for a reason. Each one matters. Each one of them is someone I love.*'

* 1 Corinthians 14:3.

As I read the list of names, I thanked God with a fresh appreciation, reminded that no one in history or today is forgotten by him. That he sees, knows and loves all.

Having said that, I also want to emphasise that while I *try* to read through the whole Bible every year, there have been times when I have missed a day, or haven't managed to read all the passages for a particular day, and I just pick up where I left off. For me it's about finding the balance between the discipline of reading the Bible every day, not getting into legalism, and not giving myself too much of a hard time on the odd occasion I miss a day or don't quite manage all the readings.

And it has been so rewarding. As I have read the whole Bible, I have found that it really does give me an understanding of the whole, sweeping and epic story of God creating us to be in relationship with him, humankind falling and failing again and again, and God's relentless love, mercy, grace and patience in seeking to draw us back to himself and providing a way for this to happen through the person of Jesus.

A SPECIAL INSIGHT

A number of our friends work in the fashion industry, and while their sense of style is inspiring, it has not rubbed off on me! I was talking to one of them, someone who designs the most beautiful clothes for a high-end brand, and she started talking enthusiastically about how God is the original Designer and Creator. 'Think about it, Bill,' she said. 'Look at creation – so diverse, so beautiful, totally original. In fashion we often take ideas and rework them, but all that we see in the natural world came from the mind of God – he created it, quite literally, from nothing.'

I could tell she was getting really excited. 'More than that – look at the design for the temple and its furnishings, and the level of detail it goes into in some of the passages in 2 Chronicles. It would have been awe-inspiring, spectacular. A place that spoke of his majesty and glory. It would have inspired devotion and worship. In fact, it was the description of the design of the priestly garments in Exodus 28 that not only convinced me how much clothing design matters to God, but was also the passage that God used to speak to me very clearly when I was really seeking him about my calling when I left university.'

I could see that this passage, that I had so often read, had had a significant impact on her life: 'I had really been praying about my future and God spoke so clearly and specifically. The most clearly he has ever spoken to me,' she paused for a moment. 'That passage changed my life.'

A SPECIFIC WORD FOR A SPECIFIC TIME

While it's never a good idea to take and apply single verses of the Bible entirely out of their context – to let the Bible fall open and point to the first verse you see – sometimes the Lord can arrest our attention with a specific verse or passage, whether for ourselves or for someone else. It may be that a reference of chapter and verse comes to mind, or a verse or phrase may simply stick in our mind as we read, or it may even seem to jump off the page and almost hit us in the face.

I was in a prayer room at Holy Trinity Brompton, during one of those brilliant slots at three in the morning, which always seems like a bad idea when the alarm clock goes off! I put on some music to worship, and as I did so, I began to sense the presence of God. Almost immediately someone came to my mind. My first question is always, 'Lord, is that you?' and based on the time it was, my experience with similar random words, and the fact that I had no reason to be thinking of that person, I thought, 'That seems to be God getting my attention.' I said, 'Lord, what do you want to say to this person?' and I was reminded of that verse in Jeremiah:

'For I know the plans I have for you,' declares the LORD, 'plans to prosper you and not to harm you, plans to give you hope and a future.'
JEREMIAH 29:11

It is a well-known verse, and I said, 'Well, Lord, I think he probably knows that. Have you got anything else?' But again, I was reminded of that verse, *'For I know the plans I have for you.'* I made a mental note of it, and promptly fell asleep for the rest of my time in the prayer room. To be honest I sort of forgot about it, until I happened to bump into him on Sunday at church.

The thought literally just came back to the front of my mind, and I said to him, 'Funny thing was I was in the prayer room at three o'clock on Thursday night, and you came to mind. I don't know if this is going to make any sense to you, but I just want to offer it to you as a thought; when you came to mind and I began to pray for you and ask God what his heart was for you, this verse came to my mind.'

He sat down and went very pale; and he said, 'Was that on Thursday night – three o'clock in the morning?'

And I said, 'Yes.'

He said, 'On Thursday night – at three o'clock in the morning – I was pacing up and down at home, thinking I'd just made the biggest career decision of my life, and that I'd committed career suicide essentially. I really felt that God told me to do it, and I was panicking, thinking I'd made a terrible mistake. The fact that when I was pacing up and down, God was speaking to you about it and reminding me of one of my favourite promises in the Bible, is really encouraging.'

So, he was encouraged, and I was encouraged through a simple verse from the Bible.

There are of course many other ways that God speaks to us, and these are also outlined in the Bible. In the next few chapters, I'm going to explore just some of them.

practise

When did you last read the Bible? What was God saying to you?

Reflect for a moment on your current practice of reading the Bible. What time of day do you read it? What are you reading in the Bible at the moment? Are you following a Bible reading plan, or working through a particular book? Are you memorizing Scripture or reading aloud or listening to a Bible app, or practising *Lectio Divina*?

If you are looking to refresh your rhythm of reading the Bible, here are a few ideas that you might like to consider.

- *The God Story*. Try reading the Bible chronologically and under-standing the overarching story of Scripture. There are a number of good chronological Bibles available, and several chronological Bible reading plans, including one developed by 24-7 Prayer called *The God Story*.

- Memorizing Scripture. Learn a Psalm or a favourite passage off by heart each morning – and bring that scripture back to mind throughout the day.

- The *Bible in a Year*.

- A book in one sitting. Many of the books of the Bible were written to be read aloud, in one sitting. Choose a letter of Paul's and read it aloud from start to finish. You could start with a short one, like Philippians, or something longer like 1 Corinthians.

- Choose a psalm, and prayerfully rewrite it in your own words, and apply your own experience.

- A weekly Bible study. If you can't manage to read the Bible every day, set aside an hour on the weekend to really study the Bible.

- Try an audio Bible and listen to it while out on a walk or on your way to work.

- Celtic daily prayer: a daily liturgy developed by the Northumbria Community is also helpful.

- *Lectio 365*: Download the 24-7 Prayer morning – or evening – prayer app and listen on your way to work.

- *Pray As You Go* – another daily Bible reading and prayer app, produced by a Jesuit group.

- Design your own. If you can't find the right plan for you, or a programme makes you feel restricted, take things into your own hands. Decide which book of the Bible you would like to read for the next month. Gather some resources to help you. Decide how much you want to read in a day and make a start.

And here are some books to help you in your Bible reading.

- *How to Read the Bible for All Its Worth* – Gordon Fee (Zondervan, 2003)

- *God's Big Picture* – Vaughan Roberts (IVP UK, 2009)

- *Search the Scriptures* – Alan Stibbs (IVP, 2004)

- *Bible Study Methods* – Rick Warren (Zondervan, 2006)

- *Why Trust the Bible?* – Amy Orr-Ewing (IVP, 2020)

- *A Passion for God's Story* – Philip Greenslade (Paternoster, 2002)

written in the sky

how God speaks through everyday places and circumstances

The earth is the LORD's, and everything in it,
 the world, and all who live in it;
for he founded it on the seas
 and established it on the waters.

PSALM 24:1-2

We all have them – places that are so familiar that they are almost a part of us. We have passed by them, over them, under them, through them or round them so many times that they have almost become a character in our story. One of mine is the Wandsworth roundabout.

I can't remember a time in my life when I didn't know the Wandsworth roundabout. The only notable change that I can think of was when McDonald's built a drive-through just beside it, and that was so long ago I can't ever remember that not being there either. As nondescript as it is, perhaps even because of this, the Wandsworth roundabout has been a reassuring constant. A place where comfort can be had knowing it is a place where nothing of consequence ever happens. A place so familiar that I almost go into a form of safe autopilot when I drive round it. There was nothing particular or unusual about that September afternoon when I drove round it, as I had done so many times before. Thoughts drifted randomly, and I hummed to the radio. And, in among the predictably familiar, a work colleague came to mind. His name was Simon.

I have to confess that I didn't know Simon at all, and had only said a cursory 'hello' to him when I'd popped downstairs to the office that he shared with a friend of mine to ask my friend if he wanted to come and get a sandwich at lunchtime. The only thing I knew about Simon was that he had been working at the church for about six months at this point.

While there was nothing particularly unusual about it as people often occupied my thoughts, it was just that this one seemed so random. I had been spending time with my friend Carl the week before and he encouraged me to notice when the random came into the familiar and push into the thought and consider where it came from – maybe God was dropping little teasers, Easter eggs, so to speak, into my mind.

So, in that moment, as I sat at the traffic lights on the Wandsworth roundabout, where I had sat so many times before, I just said, 'God, I don't know if that thought was from you, or it's because I'm just hungry, but if it is, please speak to me and help me to hear what you might be saying to Simon.'

Almost as soon as I had finished, another thought, a knowing, came to mind – that Simon felt lost – stuck between careers in a job that he didn't like, and he was wondering where God was in all of it – and whether God even knew or cared.

I drove round the roundabout again. 'Lord, if this is you, please can you give me more clarity about what it is Simon wants to do, and what you might be wanting to say to him about it,' I prayed.

Again, as I prayed, I had another knowing, another insight.

'Lord,' I said, 'I think this is you. I hope it's you. Is this something I am supposed to be praying for him, or something you want me to share with him?'

I have to admit that if it were possible to pray with all my fingers crossed while doing another circuit of the roundabout, my fingers would have been very much crossed. I didn't know Simon at all well and had had the grand total of zero one-on-one discussions with him, and it felt like going very far out on a very fragile limb to even consider the possibility of saying something to him of this nature.

Again, it seemed like an answer came back quickly. '*Call him*,' was the response. At this point I drove round the roundabout again and turned off at the McDonald's exit. Maybe I was just experiencing a sugar low, I thought. Perhaps a chocolate milkshake would help.

It didn't.

What I can only describe as a conviction seemed to be growing.

I took a big sip of my shake, called the office switchboard and asked to be put through to Simon.

The phone rang a few times.

'Hello?' said the voice at the other end.

'Hi Simon, this is Bill here. I hope you are doing okay. Is this a good moment?'

'Yes, it's fine, what can I do for you?' Simon asked.

'Simon, I was just driving to a meeting and you came to mind. A thought came to mind that might be worth sharing with you.'

'Okay,' came the reply.

'Are you sure – I'm very happy to grab a coffee with you tomorrow if you'd prefer that.'

'No, Bill, really it's fine. Go for it.'

'As I said, I was driving round the Wandsworth roundabout on the way to a meeting, and you came to mind,' I explained. 'And, no offence, it seemed so random, so I prayed and asked God if it was him trying to say something. I'm aware we don't know each other at all, so forgive me if this all seems a little invasive, but I hope you don't mind me asking, are you happy with your job, with where you are at?'

There was a short pause followed by a deep breath.

'As I said, I'm really happy to grab a coffee tomorrow if that's easier.'

'No, I'm glad you called. I don't want to say too much yet but keep going.'

'Simon, as I prayed, the sense I had was that you felt stuck between careers in a job you don't like, that really what you want to be doing is human rights law.'

I waited a few seconds.

'Simon, what I think God might be wanting to say to you is that he hasn't forgotten you. He loves you, he loves the passion you have for justice and for human rights – he put that in you, and what he is wanting to show you is that if you are patient now you will see him open doors for you that you don't think are possible.'

There was a very long silence.

'Thanks Bill,' came the eventual reply. 'That's helpful.'

'Okay,' I said. 'You know where I am if you want to chat.'

'Yep. Thanks. Speak soon,' he said before he put the phone down.

I sat there sipping my shake for a few minutes, thinking about the exchange. Had I been too pushy? Not given him enough of a chance to opt out? Should I have waited until I saw him next? What if it had all been in my head? I was just about to start the ignition in the car again when I heard my phone ping. And there was an email from Simon.

Hi Bill,

Thanks for your call. Sorry I was a bit abrupt at the end. I was trying really hard not to burst into floods of tears. You have no idea how timely your call was. It may have felt random to you, but it really meant a lot to me. I had been praying this morning and telling God how lost I felt and how confused I was as I thought he had a plan for me to be a human rights lawyer, and this job most definitely wasn't what I wanted or expected – I asked him if he saw me or even cared. While I still don't have all the answers, I know now that God does see me and does care. I'll just have to work on the being patient bit!

Let's grab that coffee soon,

Thanks again,

Simon

As I sat there thinking about the email I had just read, I was struck by how easily I could have missed the whole thing. There I was driving round the same familiar roundabout I had driven round countless times before, humming along to a song on the radio when a random thought dropped into my mind. It would have been so easy to ignore it as all just being part of the familiar. And yet God was speaking in that moment, as uneventful and familiar as the context was.

God doesn't just speak to people in church. God is speaking all the time. Often in the most familiar places. The places that we least expect him to speak. In the supermarket, at the school gate, by the printer at work, in the gym, the coffee shop, the allotment, while you are on a video conference call, and even while driving round the Wandsworth roundabout.

GOD SPEAKS THROUGH ORDINARY CIRCUMSTANCES AND FAMILIAR THINGS

'God is speaking all the time Bill,' said my friend Carl as I recounted the story to him, 'particularly in the familiar places. The places so familiar that we don't expect him to be there. He loves to hide himself in the ordinary and surprise us if only we will learn to see him and hear him there.'

Carl was right. As I thought about it, I was struck by the story of Moses in the desert. A prince of Egypt turned fugitive. Many years had passed since he fled for his life having killed an Egyptian in a moment of anger as he saw him striking a slave – one of his own people. There he was, in the wilderness, tending the flock of his father-in-law, and he sees a bush on fire. I'm not sure how common this would have been, how often, in the heat, a little plant or bush might dry to the point of combustion in that part of the desert. And yet something about that occasion caught his attention, if only for a moment. The bush kept on burning – it wasn't consumed. And that was enough to give him pause – to cause him to move towards the bush rather than carrying on. It was in the familiar, in the ordinary, the everyday, that God spoke to him and Moses received a commission that changed everything.*

Gideon asked for a sign through something familiar, something that happened every morning – the presence of dew. In the desert, because it's often so very dry, dew in the morning is a significant and a familiar feature, and everyone would know what time of year and under what conditions it tended to come. Gideon asked that the Lord would confirm his word, and that the fleece he laid out on the threshing floor would be wet the next morning and the ground dry, and he squeezed out enough water to fill a bowl. The next night, just to be sure, he asked that the ground would be wet but the fleece dry.**

Once, when I went for a job interview, I heard God speak very clearly through a simple circumstance. Initially when I applied, and on the way to the interview, I was quite excited about it. But deep down I wasn't sure whether I really wanted the job or not; I wasn't sure it was the right thing. I remember praying, saying, 'Lord, is this what you have for me?' And then as I was being shown round the school, I felt a sense of unease. Which may sound very subjective – it was a good school and a good job. But the thing that clinched it was a seemingly ordinary circumstance. The teacher who showed me round was trying to show me the classroom that would have been mine, but he couldn't get the door open, it was locked. Literally. He didn't have the key. He had a ring of keys to all the doors in the school, and was going through them, trying each of them one

* Exodus 2:11–12; Exodus 3.
** Judges 6:36–40.

by one. It was like something out of a farce. And I felt myself say, inwardly, 'Okay, I get it.' The door was closed, literally. God spoke, and I knew that even if they had offered me the job, I couldn't take it. They interviewed me, and at lunchtime they told me I had got through to the next round, but that the second stage of the interview was that afternoon, and first they'd like to know, if they offered me the job at the end of the day, whether I would be in a position to take it. All I could think about was the locked door. I withdrew.

Which might sound like a trivial example, but it was God speaking. And it was kinder than simply not being offered the job – often God allows us to participate in a decision, and to choose his way.

Abraham's servant was entrusted with a great responsibility: to find a wife for Isaac. He asked for a sign that while he was sitting by the well the right girl, the one to marry Isaac, would agree to give him a drink, and offer to water his camels also. When these seemingly ordinary events played out before him he took this as a sign that Rebekah was the one. She turned out to be from Abraham's family, and so the sign was wonderfully confirmed.*

Nicky Gumbel writes that we would be foolish if we made a decision based only on a circumstantial sign, but we would be equally foolish if we ignored it.

Circumstances can speak, and God often speaks through circumstances. But we must be careful – we can find a sign anywhere to confirm our desires, if we want to. It is often when we are not expecting it, or through things that are unexpected, that God speaks. I wanted God to speak about the job interview, but I didn't expect him to speak through a door being locked, and the guy having every other key for the building except that one. It is not going looking for them, but being aware enough, sensitive enough to his presence that we notice those moments.

---

* Genesis 24:1–27.

SIGNS OF THE TIMES

The Pharisees and Sadducees came to Jesus and tested him by asking him to show them a sign from heaven.

He replied, 'When evening comes, you say, "It will be fair weather, for the sky is red," and in the morning, "Today it will be stormy, for the sky is red and overcast." You know how to interpret the appearance of the sky, but you cannot interpret the signs of the times. A wicked and adulterous generation looks for a sign, but none will be given it except the sign of Jonah.'

MATTHEW 16:1-4

When we experience world-changing events – earthquakes and hurricanes, floods and famines, and not least a global pandemic, it is natural to ask what will happen, what God is saying. God is speaking all the time, and he can speak through anything he chooses to, so it would be wrong to assume he is not calling us back to him through these and other means. But we must be careful not to be over-hasty about applying a more specific interpretation or judgment. Jesus told the disciples to watch and be ready, but not to be deceived. He said that there will be 'wars and rumours of wars,' that 'nation will rise against nation,' and that there will be famines and earthquakes, and to keep watch, because we won't – and we can't – know on what day our Lord will come.* The most important thing is to keep close, and keep watch, to be obedient to him and to his word.

GOD SPEAKS TO US THROUGH CREATION

The heavens declare the glory of God;
  the skies proclaim the work of his hands.
PSALM 19:1

When I go for my walk in the morning to the stream, I'm constantly struck by how it's the same walk and yet different. It's different every

---

* Matthew 24:6–7, 42.

day – what an incredible creative God we have, that he has given us changing seasons. I often stand in thankful wonder at how the sun reflects on leaves or the wind blows across the field, and when I stop and allow myself to be present in that, I'm reminded that the God that we get to talk to is the God who created it all, the God of creation.

And God speaks through his creation. One day, I walked past a spruce tree and I felt God say, '*Do you want to be a spruce or an oak?*' I didn't really understand. And so, I got my phone out and looked it up and saw essentially that spruces grow quickly, but they don't last very long; whereas oaks take a long time to grow but last hundreds of years.

We live in a world that is so immediate, we want everything now – not even now: already; we want it already. Which is just not the way God works. Tim Hughes once said there are two ways that God answers prayer. Slowly or suddenly. Mostly he works slowly.

I've thought about this word, about the oak and the spruce, a lot. In fact, I think about it all the time. An oak doesn't grow up overnight. It grows slowly over a long period of time, and if you were the oak you'd say it's worth the time, because of what you will become; this majestic, mighty tree as opposed to the spruce, which people try to get rid of quickly because they self-seed and are a nuisance. I often say that to people – when they are frustrated and say they're not growing quickly enough, I'll say, 'Well, do you want to be an oak or spruce?'

GOD SPEAKS TO AND THROUGH OTHER PEOPLE

Plans fail for lack of counsel,
  but with many advisers they succeed.
PROVERBS 15:22

In other words, surround yourself with godly people because they are going to give good advice because they love God and they love you, and listen as he speaks through them. In my own experience God is often very practical and while we might want what we consider to be spiritual answers, what we often need, and what he often does, is to speak common sense to us through others.

When I first met Nici I knew within two weeks that I wanted to marry her. I'm not known for being particularly subtle, so I think it was pretty obvious early on that I was quite keen. It took me a little while to convince her that she should go out with me, but when she did, after two weeks I knew that I wanted to spend the rest of my life with this amazing woman.

The first person I spoke to was my friend Ed. Ed gave me what I thought was relatively good advice, on the face of it; but then I went away and thought about it, and I thought, 'Ed has never had a girlfriend, and I'm asking him for his advice on the most important decision of my life.' Ed suggested I write a list of all the reasons why I should marry her on one side of the page, and all the reasons why I shouldn't on the other. Now that's great if you're thinking about buying a car, but on reflection maybe not the best advice on whether you should ask someone to marry you! I love Ed, he is an amazing guy, but I thought, 'Actually, I probably need to ask someone else as well at some point.' I did do the list – the 'reasons to' side of the page was crammed. The 'reasons not to' was blank.

A week and a half later, I was on the verge of proposing to Nici. Given that I had only been going out with her for three weeks, I didn't know her all that well, but I knew her well enough to know that she would want to choose her own ring, so I had got a token shiny purple plastic ring from a gift shop in Leicester for the proposal itself.

It was a Saturday afternoon and as Nici popped into the local supermarket, I just thought, 'Let's do this. I'm going to propose to her when she comes out!'

I thought that perhaps it would be a good idea to phone my friend Ric, who not only had had a girlfriend in the past, but was actually married, to ask what he thought, so while Nici was in the shop, I gave him a quick call.

His wife Louie answered the phone, and when I asked if I could speak to Ric she said Ric had just gone out.

'I think I'm going to propose to Nici,' I told her excitedly, 'this afternoon – when she comes out of the supermarket!'

There was a pause. 'Where are you?' Louie asked.

'I'm in the car outside the Co-op in Market Harborough,' I replied.

'Ric's not here,' she said calmly, 'but can I give you two bits of advice? First of all, call back in an hour, but more importantly, whatever you do, don't do it now!'

'Okay,' I said, feeling a little dejected. 'I'll call him in an hour or so.'

Fifty-three minutes later Ric called me. He gave me some really good, really sage advice, and he asked me a couple of questions, which helped me to think through practically and biblically about what marriage was. That advice, which was mostly common sense, probably saved my marriage – before I'd even proposed!

---

practise

Next time you go out of the house, whether to buy milk from the cornershop, commute to work or to meet friends at the pub, remind yourself that the presence of God is everywhere. Ask the Lord to open your eyes to where he is working.

---

seeing visions and dreaming dreams

how God speaks through pictures

'And afterward,
  I will pour out my Spirit on all people.
Your sons and daughters will prophesy,
  your old men will dream dreams,
  your young men will see visions.'

JOEL 2:28

TATTOOS AND COATS OF ARMOUR: SEEING VISIONS

I was at a gathering, standing in a queue for something or other, and was surprised to notice that a friend ahead of me had a tattoo on the back of her neck. I didn't think anything of it, but I mentioned it to another friend I was sharing a room with, and he said that she definitely didn't have one, she wasn't a tattoo person, and I said no she definitely does, because I saw it.

The next time I saw her, the tattoo was still there, so I tried to sketch it out as best I could – it was a design of words. In the meantime, my friend had mentioned this to her, and she came up and asked me what it said. And I said I didn't know, but it looked like it was in Greek or Hebrew, and I tried to write it out as best I could and ran it through google translate. In the end I understood it to say something like 'healing in her wings.' So, I told her what I thought it said, at which point she said, 'There are two things you need to know: the first thing is I'm about to have an operation because the position of my neck is causing really bad headaches; and the second thing is, here's my business card.' And she handed it to me. It had a picture of a butterfly and said, 'healing in his wings.'

It was so real that I didn't realise it was a vision. This kind of vision is sometimes called an open vision, something you see with your eyes open, as if it was really there. For a while after that I kept seeing tattoos on people; they would be words written on their arms, or their legs, or their hands, or their forehead.

In Chapter 5 we talked about the ways we encounter the presence of God, by feeling or knowing, but also by hearing and seeing. The ways we might encounter God by seeing are either while asleep in dreams, or awake through visions.

The word 'vision' can perhaps be a little intimidating, and in British culture, where we have a tendency towards understatement, we often use the word 'picture' to refer to what might otherwise be described as a vision.

The Bible is clear, however, that God does speak to people in and through visions. Visions are best described as vivid apparitions that are most often experienced when people are awake. Examples in the Old Testament include Ezekiel, Daniel, Zechariah and the book of Revelation in the New Testament. In the book of Acts, we read about Paul having a vision of Jesus on the road to Damascus, and Ananias and Paul receiving visions to prepare Paul for baptism. Likewise,

Peter and Cornelius received visions to prepare them for Peter's ministry among the Gentiles.*

Visions or pictures might best be broken into two categories – visions that occur in our mind's eye, or 'closed visions'; and visions or pictures that are seen with our eyes as if they are real and are sometimes referred to as 'open visions'. There is not a hierarchy in terms of which might be considered a greater vision, and the Bible is often not clear whether what was seen was in the mind's eye or as an open vision.

It always amazes me how often people who are new to faith talk of having received pictures, which, when they describe them they are visual representations of passages of Scripture. I remember someone who had recently come to faith saying that he had a picture of people dressed in armour and that he sensed God reminding people that he had armour for them to wear to protect themselves.

'Have you read the book of Ephesians?' I asked.

'The book of what?' he answered.

I then explained to him how God had just given him a picture that explained a passage of scripture where Paul encourages people to put on the metaphorical armour of God to defend themselves.**

CONVICTION AND COMPASSION: DREAMING DREAMS

In the Bible there are twenty-one accounts of God speaking through dreams. What is striking about them isn't just what is said, but who it is said to. If you take a quick survey, you will notice that most of them were not heroes, not exactly the people who were God's equivalent of *Jedi* – they were actually often (although not exclusively) quite the opposite. It really is a cast of questionable characters. I find that hugely encouraging – if God speaks in dreams to people like Jacob, who cheated and lied his way to his brother's

---

* You can look up examples of visions in the Bible here: Ezekiel 37:1–10; Daniel 5:1–28; 7:1–8, 17; Acts 9:1–6, 10–19; 10:3–35.
** Ephesians 6:10–17.

inheritance, or a megalomaniacal ruler like Nebuchadnezzar, or a teenage girl from a small provincial backwater, then he can speak to you and me in dreams too!*

I have a notebook by my bed, and when I dream something, I try to wake myself up and write it down, or speak it aloud and record it on my phone. I leave it until the morning to try and work out whether it was God speaking, or just me dreaming. Often, I realise quite quickly if it was me – I might have eaten something that triggered it, or my subconscious mind might be trying to process something. While it might be those things, it might also be God, and it is often only in hindsight that I really begin to discern which it is.

That is why keeping a record can be so helpful. When reviewing my dreams I might think about the last few dreams, and reflect on what they all involve or have in common – is a theme emerging? Is there a pattern? Is it an encouragement, challenge or a warning? Who or what are the common threads? Does it, or do they, reveal something of the nature and character of God as revealed in the Bible?

Dreams can bring strong conviction. Once I had a dream about an attitude that I had but wasn't consciously aware of. In the dream I saw myself reacting to something someone said, and instantly, as I woke, got straight on my knees and asked for forgiveness and help to overcome that attitude, because what I saw in that dream was something I was not proud of. I've also had dreams where God has clearly spoken to me about other people. If, after spending some time discerning whether it is something to share, I tell them, it has often been humbling and moving to hear what the dream has meant to the person or people concerned.

One of these occasions was during a conference. After the end of the first day, that night, I had a dream of a young couple weeping as they put a teddy bear into a cardboard box. As is often the case, we can tend to jump to conclusions, and, because I didn't know who the couple was, I initially assumed that perhaps they had

---

* Genesis 28; Daniel 2; Luke 1:26–38.

had a pregnancy that hadn't gone to term and that the baby had died. I woke up to find that I too was weeping. I felt a small part of the sadness I imagined they must be feeling, and a huge sense of compassion for them.

The following morning, before the conference started, I talked to a trusted friend about the dream. When I had finished, he looked at me and said, 'What did the Lord say when you asked him what it meant?'

I looked at him a bit sheepishly. 'I haven't asked him about it.'

'Bill, do you remember in Jeremiah Chapter 1, when Jeremiah has a vision. God said to him, "Jeremiah, what do you see?" I don't know if you have ever thought about it, but God already knew what Jeremiah had seen, because he was the one who put the vision in his head in the first place!'

I must have looked a little confused.

'Bill,' he said, 'God was wanting to draw him into a conversation. That's what relationship is. God is always wanting to draw us deeper into friendship with him. Maybe he's trying to do the same with you through this dream. Ask him what the dream is about – don't be in a rush, let him speak to you in his time – you might be surprised.'

As I thought about what my friend said, I began to ask God what the dream meant. As I did, I was reminded of a passage in Isaiah:

'For my thoughts are not your thoughts,
  neither are your ways my ways,'
  declares the LORD.
'As the heavens are higher than the earth,
  so are my ways higher than your ways
  and my thoughts than your thoughts.'
ISAIAH 55:8–9

I immediately felt encouraged. It was as if God was saying that he loved that I was coming to him, that he wanted me to press into him, and also gently remind me that he might be wanting to say something different to what I had assumed.

'Okay, Lord,' I prayed. 'Please help me to move beyond my assumptions, to a place where I know your thoughts and your heart more clearly.'

Over the course of the day, the more I prayed for this couple, who I didn't know, the more it seemed that my discernment about the dream started to shift. What I came to understand was so different from what I had initially assumed. I still wasn't clear whether this was something I was supposed to share with the couple, so again I began to ask. As I did, and as I discussed the dream and what it might mean pastorally with a good friend, I was reminded again and again of what Paul wrote to the Corinthian church when he sought to encourage them to keep pressing into prophecy:

> *Follow the way of love and eagerly desire gifts of the Spirit, especially*
> *prophecy. For anyone who speaks in a tongue does not speak to people*
> *but to God. Indeed, no one understands them; they utter mysteries*
> *by the Spirit. But the one who prophesies speaks to people for their*
> *strengthening, encouraging and comfort.*
>
> 1 CORINTHIANS 14:1-3

It was the first and last sentences that seemed to lodge themselves in my brain. 'Follow the way of love ... the one who prophesies speaks to people for their strengthening, encouraging and comfort.' To love this couple was to share the dream and my understanding of it with them sensitively with words that might strengthen, encourage and comfort them.

There was a time of prayer at the end of the second day, and so I stood at the front of the church and briefly shared the very bare minimum so as not to make the couple feel exposed in any way, while saying enough so that the couple would know that it was them. 'I had a dream last night about a couple who are longing for a family. If that resonates with you, I'd love to meet you and pray with you. I'll be standing just at the side of the room if you want to come and talk,' I said, and then went to wait.

As the session came to an end, I noticed a couple lingering nearby. I could tell that they were waiting to talk to me, but perhaps were understandably nervous. I caught their eye, smiled and motioned for them to follow me into a more discreet room beside the main hall.

We sat down with a coffee and I started sharing the dream with them. I had spent a fair amount of time thinking about what I was going to say – it was just too sensitive and too important to make it up on the spot. And I remembered one of the things that my friend Carl had said to me once, that the most important thing is to help people feel safe, to give them space, and time, to respond. If they didn't want to hear any more, that would be totally fine. My job was to offer the dream and then ask if they wanted to hear a bit more, or if they wanted to leave it there.

'I don't know if the dream means anything to you,' I said as I concluded recounting it to them, 'and I totally understand if you would rather leave it there.'

The couple looked at each other – I could tell just from looking at them that they were experiencing a range of emotions. The husband took a searching look into his wife's eyes; she nodded. 'It's fine, Bill, keep going.'

I paused. In that moment they were inviting me into something very private and precious.

'As I've thought and prayed about this dream, the sense I have is that you have longed for a baby for a long time – and that you feel like you have exhausted your options and that you have lost hope, that it's just too painful to keep going down this path.'

I paused again and they both started weeping.

'I can't imagine how hard and how painful this must be for you,' I continued slowly, 'and what I want to encourage you with is that the sense I have is that God wants you to know he is with you; in your confusion, your anger and your pain, he wants you to know that he is closer than you think.'

They were both sobbing now – deep, deep tears and groans – it was as if all the pain that they had been feeling for so long between themselves was coming to the surface.

'I have thought really hard about what I want to say next, and I don't say it lightly,' I paused again. 'But I wonder if God might be inviting you to trust him one last time. I'm not sure what that means, or what it might look like. I know it would be putting yourselves out there again and risking the pain all over again. I know it's so easy for me to say, and so much harder for you to do, but if you would like, I would love to pray with you.'

They nodded between their tears, holding each other tight.

'Father,' I prayed slowly, tears starting to roll down my own cheeks too, 'we don't understand why this has happened. Right now, it feels raw and painful. We know that you promise that you are good, and we ask that you help this couple to hold onto you, to trust you one more time. We're not sure what that means, but we ask that you show them. Mostly we pray that they would know that you are with them. Amen.'

We sat in the room together for a few minutes, hugged and I wished them well as they disappeared into the throng of other guests heading out from the conference into the summer's evening.

As I stood there I thought again about the kindness of God – that he would speak to a stranger in a dream and use it as a way of reaching out and showing a couple visiting London for a conference that he was with them in the midst of their situation.

As I walked into the church office one autumn morning the receptionist stopped me and said, 'Bill, there is a lady here to see you.'

'Hi,' I said, as I walked towards her. 'I'm Bill, how can I help?'

'You probably don't remember me, but I was at the conference the church ran last year. I was here with my husband. You said you had a dream, and we came, and you prayed with us at the end of the second day.'

I remembered her instantly.

'Yes, of course!' I said, not quite sure what to expect next. 'How are you both?'

'We are very well,' she said. 'That conference changed our lives for many reasons … and our conversation about your dream and the time of prayer we had was so helpful. It was still hard, but we left deciding to trust God one last time, and I'd like you to meet someone,' she smiled as she stood to one side. 'This is our daughter. She was born ten months after the conference. Her name is Hope.'

WATCHING OVER US

Angels occupy a very particular place in our religious heritage and the western cultural landscape. We don't have to look far for examples, whether the great works of art by Raphael, Leonardo da Vinci and Caravaggio, music by Bach, Mozart, Sarah McLachlan or Robbie Williams, films such as *City of Angels*, *Down to Earth* or *Angels on the Outfield*, or TV programmes like *Angels and Demons* or *Highway to Heaven*. I think that they have grown in popular cultural consciousness in part because the thought of being protected by divine heavenly beings brings comfort and hope that we are not alone, particularly in difficult and challenging times.

Someone I know well had a very real experience with heavenly beings.

'My wife was away on a trip abroad for an event; in all the time we'd been married it was the longest we'd ever been apart. Halfway through her time away I was really missing her. I was upstairs about to go to bed, and I was praying for her. Then I looked across the room, and through the side of the wall and the roof, this figure came through the side of the house, and stopped and hovered, looking at me. It was one of those experiences where, I have to confess, I did wonder if I was experiencing some kind of psychotic episode.

I slapped myself on the face just to make sure that I wasn't actually asleep and dreaming it all, only to find that yes, I was awake, my face was now hurting, and I was looking at what I could only assume was an angel. It looked at me for what must have been a few seconds, smiled kindly, turned and disappeared the way it came.

I stood in our room stunned, "Lord, what just happened? Why did it happen?"

As soon as I prayed, I felt him say, "It's now going to check on Lisa." I felt so known and so loved in that moment.

I didn't tell anyone for years because I felt embarrassed and self-conscious about it. I wondered if people would believe me, and what they would think.'

When I asked my friend Carl about angels, he said, 'Bill, I think there are angels everywhere – it's just most of us don't see them, don't perceive them because we are so caught up in what is happening, and every now and again some of us get to see what is already there and happening around us all the time. I don't know why some people see them, and why others don't, but what is important to remember is that it is a reminder that God is always present, always at work, and that he is always, always good.'

There are 290 references to angels in the Bible, and angels perform many roles, very often as divine messengers, whether that is to bring comfort and guidance to Hagar in the desert, rescue to Lot, calling and destiny to Moses or insight to Zechariah.[*]

Angelic activity is at the centre of the nativity narratives and indeed some of the key moments in Jesus' life – appearing to Mary to explain what is about to happen, to Joseph to counsel him to take Mary home as his wife, to bewildered shepherds to announce Jesus' birth, and later to warn Joseph of Herod's intentions and to tell Joseph and Mary to escape to Egypt before finally letting them

---

[*] Genesis 16:1–15; Genesis 19; Exodus 3:2; Luke 1:5–25.

know it is safe to return home after the death of Herod some time later. Later in the life of Jesus we read of angels ministering to Jesus in the wilderness after he has been tempted by the devil, as he struggled in prayer in the Garden of Gethsemane prior to his arrest and crucifixion, and finally when Jesus had been resurrected, to tell Mary Magdalene and Mary that Jesus was now alive.*

There are numerous accounts of angelic activity throughout history, which again tell a story of divine messengers sent by God to speak hope, comfort or encouragement, or to bring divine protection. In his love, it seems God will often send angels to the alone, the afraid, the vulnerable, the confused or those in need of courage.

The message is clear. You are not alone. I am with you.

---

practise

Ask God to give you dreams. Keep a notebook by your bed and write down your dreams when you wake. After a couple of weeks read through them and see if there is a pattern or a theme emerging. Ask God to help you understand what he is saying to you through your dreams.

---

* Luke 1:26–38; 2:9–15; Matthew 1:20; 2:13; 4:11; Luke 22:43; John 20:12.

CHAPTER 9

great and unsearchable things

God speaks through the gift of words of knowledge

'Call to me and I will answer you and tell you great and unsearchable things you do not know.'

JEREMIAH 33:3

AN (EXTRA)ORDINARY SUNDAY EVENING

I don't know what Sunday evenings are like in your family, but when we lived in London there always seemed to be a moment of realisation at about 8:45pm that the food we had bought for our boys' packed lunches for the first half of the week seemed mysteriously to have been eaten over the weekend. This would lead to a quick dash to the supermarket before it closed at 9pm.

I was on my way home from work one Sunday evening when Nici called and asked if I could stop by the supermarket to pick up a few things for at least Monday's lunches.

I was listening to a talk about someone who had grown in recognising God's voice in his ordinary everyday life to such an extent that it was having a significant impact on the people he met. It reminded me of Brent Rue's talk on intimacy with God which had had made such an impression on me in the first few months of my coming to faith. And what I was hearing now was like a supercharged version of that. People were quite literally encountering the love of God wherever he went, and I found myself quite stirred by the thought – what might it look like if that happened in my life? Forgive me if it sounds pretentious, but one thing that really motivates me is a desire for people to realise that they are seen, known and loved by God, and this is what was happening everywhere this man went.

'Yes, Lord, this is what I want,' I prayed as I listened to the talk. 'Bring it on!'

I pulled up outside the supermarket, went in and loaded a basket with things I thought the boys would like for lunch the next day, and joined the queue of other people who had obviously had a similar thought.

Perhaps it was because I still had that talk buzzing round my head, but as I stood there in the supermarket queue I began, just faintly, to become aware of the presence and goodness of God – it wasn't so much a feeling as a knowing. I just *knew* he was there.

One of the things I've learned over the years, is to say to God in those moments, 'Lord, thank you that you are here. Why are you here? Is there anything you want to remind me of, or say to me?' So, as I stood there, I began to ask those questions. By this stage I was now standing at the till and a young woman was scanning my shopping. It was at that point that a thought came quite literally out of nowhere:

'*She's a singer.*'

'That's nice,' I thought. And then I remembered the time I had been driving around the Wandsworth roundabout and realised the thought about my work colleague had come to mind in the same way.

The thought came again, this time more strongly, 'She's a singer.' I could feel my heart rate starting to increase. 'What now?' I thought. There it was again, 'She's a singer.' I paused, took a deep breath, 'Excuse me,' I said as she continued to scan my items (and my heart was beating really quite fast now), 'I hope you don't mind me asking, but are you a singer?'

She paused for a moment and looked at me, slightly confused. 'Yes?' she said. To be honest I wasn't quite sure if she was making a statement or asking a question.

I felt a strange mixture of relief combined with a 'What now?'

We stood there both slightly uncertain for a moment and before I had time to work out what to say next, another thought came:

'She's a singer in a choir.'

I'm not sure if you have ever found yourself in a situation where you have been caught off guard and the world seems to slow down while your brain simultaneously speeds up, but that is how I felt in that moment. Along with having to admit that I was the one who put myself in the situation in the first place.

At the same time, although I had never found myself in a situation exactly like this before – standing at the supermarket checkout on a Sunday evening and encountering both the presence of God and the voice of God – I told myself that since I had asked the first question and it had been right, perhaps if God was speaking, I should just turn what I'd received into another question.

'Are you a singer in a choir?' I enquired, slightly less nervously than the first time.

Her eyes narrowed somewhat, not so much in anxiety or fear, but more out of a sense, I suspected, of trying to work out what was happening.

'Yes, I am,' she replied.

'Sweet relief!' I thought, at which point a third thought came:

'She's a singer in a choir in a church.'

By this stage my thought process, or at least what was left of it, was, 'Okay, let's just keep going – two out of two isn't a bad average.'

'I'm so sorry,' I said as gently as I could, not wanting to put her on the spot or make her feel any more uncomfortable than she probably was feeling already. 'Are you a singer in a choir in church?' I asked.

'Yes, I am ... Have we met somewhere before?' she asked, which seemed to be a wholly reasonable question.

I could tell that the atmosphere had begun to shift somewhat – she seemed to have moved from uncertainty to interest.

'No, I don't think so,' I replied, at which point I began to receive a fuller and more detailed knowing about her and her life.

'How do you know this stuff?' she asked, with a genuinely inquisitive look on her face.

'I'm a Christian, and I think that God might have something he wants to share with you if you'd like to hear it. If not, I totally understand – I don't want to put you any more on the spot than you already are.'

She looked at me for a moment. I could tell she was trying to size me and the whole situation up, which is exactly what I would have done if a stranger had started asking me questions while I was trying to do my job.

'Okay.'

For the first time in this exchange, which had probably lasted no more than thirty seconds, I became aware of the queue of people behind me. There were two people waiting, who, as I looked round, pretended unconvincingly to be minding their own business. One of them was peering at a newspaper, which he was holding upside down.

'I'm aware that this is a bit awkward,' I said quietly, 'and I don't know if this will make any sense to you at all, but I think that perhaps God might be wanting you to know that he knows how hard things are at home, and that you aren't sure where you fit into your mum's new family, if you do at all, but God wants you to know that he sees your tears. He's with you when you retreat to your room and write songs as an outlet and to bring comfort. Keep writing those songs – he loves them – he loves the way you come up with melodies and harmonies. How you hum them and record them on your phone.'

I paused, aware of the tears rolling down her cheeks, and not wanting to expose her or embarrass her.

'Is any of this making any sense at all?' I asked.

She stood there, tears now pouring down her cheeks. 'Yes,' she replied. 'So much sense.'

'You know something?' I asked her gently, 'Whatever happens, he will never abandon you – he loves you so much and he wants you to know that he is always, always with you.'

The queue behind me had gone very quiet.

As I looked round briefly, the man had put his newspaper down and was openly listening in on our conversation. The lady standing behind him was quietly weeping into a tissue.

'Thank you, thank you so much,' the young woman behind the checkout kept repeating. She was beaming now. 'You have no idea how much this means to me. Thank you.'

I paid and walked out of the shop as if this kind of thing happened to me every day of the week. Inside my head was spinning, a mixture of relief, elation and a feeling of humility that in those few brief moments I had been given the privilege of stepping into that young woman's life and sharing some hope with her.

'Excuse me,' said a voice behind me as I opened my car door. It was the lady who had been in the queue crying into her tissue. 'Thank you – that was one of the most extraordinary and moving things I have ever seen. It was beautiful. I've never really thought much about God, but if he or she is anything like the way you describe, that gives me hope.'

It was worth the initial awkwardness. It was worth stepping out and taking a risk. God is always good. His heart is always for us, particularly for those who are struggling.

When I got home and told Nici what had happened, she smiled, and said, 'That's great Bill, that's great. Now, the kids need to go to bed.' It was just what I needed.

WORDS OF KNOWLEDGE IN SCRIPTURE

Paul mentions the gift of a word of knowledge when he lists the gifts of the Holy Spirit in 1 Corinthians 12:8. It is distinct from a gift of a word of wisdom, and it means literally a gift of a word of knowing, and refers to knowledge given by the Holy Spirit, not ordinary human knowledge. This is the only place it is specifically named, but we see the gift of words of knowledge often being used in Scripture.

Jesus' interaction with the Samaritan woman at the well in John Chapter 4 is another example. He asks her to help him, to draw him a drink of water, and then in the exchange that follows he makes a series of comments and observations, one after another, each somehow stirring something in her, touching her curiosity and her heart and revealing more of her story each time, culminating with him telling her 'everything she ever did,' and many in the town becoming believers. He doesn't reveal everything he knows until she's engaged in the conversation and, when he does, he gives her the equivalent of a 'get out of jail free' card.

It's worth re-reading and reflecting on this story for a moment – you will find it in John 4:4–42 – and noticing a few things.

- Firstly, in the culture in which this interaction took place men and women did not engage in one-to-one discussion, neither in public nor in private.
- Secondly, she is a Samaritan: the history between Jews and Samaritans is long, complicated and both religiously and culturally fraught. At the time any travelling Jew – far more a rabbi – would avoid the entire region.

○ Thirdly, the time of day, midday, when the sun would have been at its hottest was not when most people went to draw water. So, it is possible that this is a woman who has chosen to go to the well alone, when others are likely to be elsewhere, sheltering from the heat.

○ Fourthly, Jesus *asks her* for help.

And so, this is an unusual, uncomfortable, almost dangerous situation. The woman is possibly compromised and defensive. The patience and kindness with which Jesus addresses her is breathtaking. He's God; he knows everything about her, and he doesn't embarrass her, or expose her straight away – he affords her great dignity.

He suggests, 'Go, call your husband.' At this point Jesus is touching a point of pain and shame with a seemingly innocent – or culturally appropriate – suggestion. He seems to be gently but firmly acknowledging the 'elephant in the room', the compromising situation they are in.

She could have avoided the issue, and gone off home, and we would never have read the story. But she is drawn in, wants to continue the conversation, and so partially sidesteps it; she seems to trust him enough to respond with a half-truth, one that is technically accurate: 'I have no husband.' But she walks right into it, when Jesus reveals what he already knows: 'You are right when you say you have no husband. The fact is, you have had five husbands, and the man you now have is not your husband. What you have just said is quite true.'

He speaks with kindness, compassion and directness, and the information and detail of her life that he eventually addresses could only have been revealed by the Holy Spirit.

Nathaniel is another example.[*] When Jesus first meets him, his opening line is, 'Here truly is an Israelite in whom there is no deceit.' Given that it is an unusual introduction, Nathaniel is perhaps

---

[*] John 1:47–48.

understandably somewhat bemused and asks, 'How do you know me?' Jesus' reply, again, reveals an insight he could not have known unless it was divinely revealed: 'I saw you while you were still under the fig tree before Philip called you.'

PRAY A PRAYER, ASK A QUESTION

As I think back on that evening at the supermarket, all that had really happened was that I'd prayed a prayer and I'd asked a question. And when she answered that question, I asked another one, and when she answered that, I asked another one, always giving her an 'out', so she could say no. I checked in with her when she started to cry. I talked quietly and sensitively, smiling as much as I could, and, perhaps most importantly, given the context, I kept it short.

The other thing that has often struck me is that in that moment, and others since, God has given me just enough to step out in faith without it feeling like a huge risk, and then, as I have stepped out, he has given me a bit more, and then a bit more – so that when I look back, I see a completed puzzle, made up of the small pieces that have fitted together, one piece at a time. Perhaps it's just me, but I'm not sure I would have had the confidence or, frankly, the skill and sensitivity, to manage the situation well if I had had all the jigsaw pieces at the start.

In my own journey I've learned a process that I practise if I ever find myself in a situation where I think God might have something to share with somebody: One of my first questions is, 'Lord, what do you love about them?' This is a really great question to ask. As you allow God to speak, you immediately get an insight into his heart for things about them. What he sees in them. I often follow this up by asking, 'Lord, what matters to them?' Another good question is, 'Lord, what do they like doing?'

The reason I do this is because then I can ask a question that I have a degree of confidence I may half know the answer to. The reason I ask these questions is because it helps me to begin to see them the way God does, to hold a little bit of his heart for them, and then I will frame questions around what he has revealed about the person.

An example of this could be along the following lines: I am with someone and I begin to become aware of his particular presence, and so I might begin to press into the moment – to begin to ask God what he loves about them, and what I receive as I try to encounter his voice and his love for that person is that he loves the way that they care for old people. The question I would then ask would be along the lines of, 'Do you interact much with old people?'

The reason I lead with questions rather than statements is because it gives them a way out of the conversation if they feel uncomfortable or just don't want to engage; it also gives me an 'out' because I may be wrong – I am not the oracle, and it is an adventure of faith and relationship. That said, there have been one or two occasions when people have asked me why I ask, and I might say that they seem like a very caring person. On one occasion I told the person I was with, who I knew well, that I was trying to learn to encounter God's voice for people a bit better. 'I'm really sorry – I'm making a bit of a mess of it,' I apologised. 'Yes, you are,' answered my friend laughing. 'But good on you for having a go!'

If I ask God what they like doing, and I get a feeling, or knowing, or I see a picture in my mind's eye, or hear the still small voice that they like ice skating, I might say, 'Can I ask a question – have you ever been ice skating?'

This is where framing a question is really important. If you frame it properly, if you ask a question well, it's amazing how you can get people to talk in a way that's honouring and they feel able to reveal things, without feeling like you're 'fishing' – and no one likes to feel they are the object of a fishing expedition, far less a spiritual one! The purpose of a word of knowledge, much like prophecy in general, is to use something divinely revealed about someone in such a way that they feel that they are seen, known and greatly loved by God in order to draw them into an encounter with Jesus – either in the moment or at a later date on their own.

IMPRESSIONS, KNOWING AND A GIFT OF DISCERNMENT

Finally, one of the ways God speaks to us is *through an impression.* Several times, after Jesus has cast out a demon or healed someone, some suspected him, wanting to test him. But Scripture records that Jesus knew their thoughts.* In a similar, but slightly different way, Luke records Paul taking leave of the Ephesian elders: 'And now, compelled by the Spirit, I am going to Jerusalem, not knowing what will happen to me there. I only know that in every city the Holy Spirit warns me that prison and hardships are facing me.'**

In the last chapter we talked about the different ways that we encounter the presence of God. It's more than a feeling; it's a knowing, a conviction, a deep certainty that God has spoken to you.

An impression, you could also say, is like supernatural discernment. When we explored the ways that we typically experience the presence of God in Chapter 5, one of them was 'knowing'. Another way of expressing this might be saying someone has a God-given gift of intuitive discernment.

While this is perhaps one of the more subjective ways that people encounter the presence and voice of God, it is no less powerful. But what does it look like in practice? How do you know if you are a knower?

The best way I know of to tell whether someone is a 'knower' or not is to ask if they often find that they have a sense about somebody, and it doesn't matter how many times they try and explain, everybody else just looks at them blankly, and then they quite often feel, wrongly, that they're judging the person. The reason why others don't know it is because they haven't had the revelation a knower has

---

* See for example Matthew 9:4; 12:25; Luke 11:17.
** Acts 20:22–23.

had. Often if you're a knower and you have that impression, it'll be that you understand the motivation behind what someone is doing at a deep level.

MORE THAN INTUITION

It's important to distinguish between an impression or knowing given by the Holy Spirit, and natural human intuition or perception. Over the years I have met people who are unusually perceptive about people. They just notice things about people that many of us might miss. Someone might walk in the room, not say a word, and these people just know how they're feeling, and will know what's going on, just because they have incredible powers of perception. Part of this is a God-given gift, but we need to be able to discern the difference between that – essentially reading somebody and reading somebody's soul, so to speak – and encountering God's heart for them through the Holy Spirit.

A couple of years ago I went to a prophetic gathering, and the person leading it knew that this was an area I was moving in, and they also knew that quite a few other people in the room knew me. Our children were young, and work was very busy – I walked through the door and I was just exhausted, I flopped into my chair. As the meeting started, he said, 'Bill, why don't you stand up?' So, I stood up.

He said, 'Bill, I just sense the Lord saying that you're tired. He's saying life is full on at the moment, but that it won't last forever … he promises that even the youth get tired and weary but those who hope in the Lord will find their strength, so the Lord is encouraging you to hope in him and he'll renew your strength.'

While what he had shared was a fairly innocuous statement and a Bible verse that was meant to encourage me, I felt manipulated. I didn't feel loved, I didn't feel encouraged; obviously that is the sort of thing Jesus would say because it's from the Bible, but I didn't think he'd say it like that. I was pretty sure from the looks I was getting from other people that everybody else in the room also knew what was going on, which was that in order to impress other people in the room, he'd picked out somebody that most people knew and vaguely respected, and basically was saying 'look how good I am'.

I left feeling slightly violated. There were two nights of the gathering, and I didn't go back for the second night – in fact I left at the coffee break during that first session.

I emailed the man who had got me to my feet and shared his 'word' with me and said I'd love to talk to him about what happened. When we met, I said to him, 'I want you to know I really respect you, I think you're a phenomenal prophetic voice, I've learned a lot from you, but I think it's important that you understand what my experience was when you shared with me in front of everyone the other day.'

I was respectful as I spoke. 'Mate, I didn't feel very honoured as you spoke to me. Anybody in that room, whether they'd ever heard God's voice or not, could have told me that I was tired – it was quite obvious to everyone that I was tired. So, when you said that, it didn't come across to me that it was God speaking. If I was being honest, it came across, to me at least, that you just took one look at me, read my soul, saw that I was weary and just made it into something more. I left feeling like I had been used and somewhat played.' I could see from his reaction that he understood. 'I'm telling you this because I love you and I respect you and I want to honour you by talking to you about it, so that you don't do it again.'

It couldn't have been easy to hear. I remembered when I had been challenged myself. It left me with a feeling of being found out, but also someone wanting and believing in me to do better. I hoped that this was doing the same.

To his credit, he looked me straight in the eye and replied, 'You know what – I'm really sorry. I felt a little bit insecure because there were lots of people there that I knew and respected, and I just thought I needed to pull a rabbit out of the hat at the beginning –

you got caught up in that and I'm sorry. I put myself in performance mode.'

I told him I wasn't going to come to the second week but, from what I gather, in that second week he apologised for what had happened in the gathering, and he told the people there that we'd met and talked about it and that he'd apologised to me. While he hadn't needed to do that, and I certainly hadn't asked him to, he had owned what happened and done what he could to make it right. I respected that, and him, so much for it.

AN ORDINARY SUNDAY EVENING

I want to finish this chapter on an honest note. One of my reflections is that often when we read books like this one, as brilliant and encouraging as they are, they can sometimes read like a Greatest Hits album: All the number one singles and none of the ones that crashed out of the charts almost as soon as they were released.

With that in mind I want to finish with a story where things didn't go well. At all.

About six months after the exchange with the young woman at the supermarket that I shared earlier in the chapter, I was at another supermarket on a Sunday evening a bit further from home, and again I sensed God starting to speak to me about the man behind the till.

I was really tired, I was in a real rush, and all I wanted to do was to get home. It's a terrible thing to admit but in my arrogance, I thought, 'I just don't want to do this right now, and I sort of feel like we've done this before.'

However, I decided to at least have a go, so I looked at the man in question, and I said, 'Forgive me for asking, but are you a dancer?'

He looked at me and said, 'Yeah.'

In Romans 12:6 Paul writes, 'If your gift is prophesying, then prophesy in accordance with your faith.'

As the man responded to my somewhat reluctant enquiry, my faith just went through the floor; it disappeared, I suddenly felt super self-conscious, and a little bit stupid, so I said, 'Oh, I was just wondering. Have a nice evening, goodbye,' and I drove home.

When I got home, I told Nici what had happened. She looked at me and said, 'Bill, what were you thinking?' I shrugged and said, 'I was just tired and not in the mood.'

'You need to get back in the car, drive back to the supermarket and find that man, and do him the decency of giving him your best self and your best take on what you felt like God wanted to say to him.'

I looked at her, simultaneously slightly regretting telling her but knowing she was right, even if I wasn't thrilled about the thought of it. The drive back to the supermarket seemed to take an age, but when I got there I took a deep breath and went in to find the man.

He was not behind the checkout.

'Excuse me,' I said to the person who had replaced him. 'I was just looking for the man who was here about half an hour ago. Do you know where I might be able to find him?'

'He's finished his shift and gone home, mate.'

I got that sinking feeling in the pit of my stomach. If only I had pushed past my own discomfort and attitude. What had I been thinking? Maybe God might have done something in that man's life. I was frustrated with myself for not making the most of the opportunity – and also with my own attitude which I realised had not been great. That thought, 'I just sort of feel like we've done this before,' played loudly in my mind. I had been quite happy to tell people the other supermarket story, and yet, when presented with another opportunity to reach out to someone and share what I had begun to sense was a word of knowledge for them, I had let myself get in the way. I left the supermarket frustrated with the situation and that 'What if?' feeling ruminating through me.

We will never know what might have happened had I got over myself, stepped out and trusted God and engaged in a conversation, but I have taken three learnings from it:

Firstly, God doesn't just speak to us or want to use us when we are full of faith – he speaks to us when we are tired, when we just want to go home and our attitude isn't what it might be, because his heart is to use us in the process of showing people that he sees them, knows them and loves them, and wants to draw close to people.

Secondly, I decided on the drive home, which seemed even longer than the drive back to the supermarket, that I was never going to take God speaking to me about someone else for granted again. It is always the greatest of privileges that the creator of the universe chooses to share great and unsearchable things that we do not know* and uses us to reach out to and speak into someone's life, whether they are a friend or a stranger.

Thirdly, that love is not always easy. It requires us to simultaneously put ourselves in the trajectory of someone's life, while also trying to get out of the way. We need to decide to put love on. Because when we do, we will be reminded again, that while faith, hope and love remain, the greatest of these is love. And it never fails.**

---

practise

○ Next time you meet someone new, try asking the Lord, 'Lord, what do you love about this person?' Allow God to speak, and to give you an insight into his heart for them.

○ Follow this up by asking, 'Lord, what matters to them?' or 'Lord, what do they like doing?'

○ Turn this into an opportunity to pray for them.

---

* Jeremiah 33:3.
** Colossians 3:14; 1 Corinthians 13:13; 13:8.

the still small voice and thundering

when God speaks with an audible voice

And after the fire came a gentle whisper. When Elijah heard it, he pulled his cloak over his face and went out and stood at the mouth of the cave. Then a voice said to him, 'What are you doing here, Elijah?'

1 KINGS 19:12–13

You'll notice that up to now I've tried to avoid using the word 'hear' with the voice of God. That's because 'to hear' implies perceiving the audible voice of God – and there are so many ways that God speaks. And yet, we *can* also hear God with our sense of hearing.

THE GIFT OF TONGUES

We don't know exactly what it looked or sounded like to the confused onlookers, but we can get a bit of an idea – some of Jesus' closest friends seeming inebriated first thing in the morning. Whatever it was, I suspect, given how it is described in the book of Acts, it wasn't very dignified or very quiet.

When the day of Pentecost came, they were all together in one place. Suddenly a sound like the blowing of a violent wind came from heaven and filled the whole house where they were sitting. They saw what seemed to be tongues of fire that separated and came to rest on each of them. All of them were filled with the Holy Spirit and began to speak in other tongues as the Spirit enabled them.

Now there were staying in Jerusalem God-fearing Jews from every nation under heaven. When they heard this sound, a crowd came together in bewilderment, because each one heard their own language being spoken. Utterly amazed, they asked: 'Aren't all these who are speaking Galileans? Then how is it that each of us hears them in our native language? Parthians, Medes and Elamites; residents of Mesopotamia, Judea and Cappadocia, Pontus and Asia, Phrygia and Pamphylia, Egypt and the parts of Libya near Cyrene; visitors from Rome (both Jews and converts to Judaism); Cretans and Arabs – we hear them declaring the wonders of God in our own tongues!' Amazed and perplexed, they asked one another, 'What does this mean?'

ACTS 2:1-12

I was in a prayer meeting once when someone said, 'I feel like I have a message in another tongue from God, so I'm just going to say it, and somebody here might have the interpretation.' So, he spoke the message out, and someone else there, David, immediately said, 'Do you speak Hebrew?'

He didn't, so David said, 'Well you have just spoken Hebrew; you said the beginning of Psalm 1 in Hebrew!' The person who received the tongue didn't speak Hebrew – but of course God does. As for David, Hebrew was his favourite language; he'd studied ancient Hebrew and that psalm was very pertinent for him. So it was encouraging for the person who gave the tongue, for David who loved Hebrew, and everyone else in the room as they saw the event unfold.

The gift of tongues is one that has caused great controversy in the church at different times, and Paul devotes a good deal of space to prophecy and tongues in 1 Corinthians 14. On the one hand, it is simply a heavenly language that is given to us for different reasons: there's tongues for use in private prayer and building up the spirit, for when we don't have words to pray, and there is singing in tongues for worship.* But there are times when God gives someone a message in tongues, in another language, either a human language that they don't know, or a spiritual language that they can't know. If it's a human language, quite often someone else in the room will have a translation for it quickly, as David did, because they speak the language! If it's a heavenly language, someone will be given the interpretation, and Paul directs that a public meeting should wait for the interpretation to be given.

On the day of Pentecost, there was another miracle. Only days earlier, Peter had been afraid to admit to even knowing Jesus, and the disciples were locked in a room for fear of the Jews. But when the Holy Spirit was poured out on the disciples, Peter stood up and spoke openly to the crowd who are trying to make sense of what they are seeing and hearing. He gives an extempore sermon, witnessing to the gospel. Sometimes the Lord gives us the ability to speak.

Peter quotes a passage from the book of Joel to explain what is happening:

> *"'In the last days, God says,*
> *I will pour out my Spirit on all people.*
> *Your sons and daughters will prophesy,*
> *your young men will see visions,*
> *your old men will dream dreams.*
> *Even on my servants, both men and women,*
> *I will pour out my Spirit in those days,*
> *and they will prophesy.'"*

ACTS 2:17–18

A STILL SMALL VOICE

> *The LORD said, 'Go out and stand on the mountain in the presence of the LORD, for the LORD is about to pass by.'*

---

* 1 Corinthians 12:8–10.

121

Then a great and powerful wind tore the mountains apart and shattered the rocks before the Lord, but the Lord was not in the wind. After the wind there was an earthquake, but the Lord was not in the earthquake. After the earthquake came a fire, but the Lord was not in the fire. And after the fire came a gentle whisper. When Elijah heard it, he pulled his cloak over his face and went out and stood at the mouth of the cave.

Then a voice said to him, 'What are you doing here, Elijah?'
1 KINGS 19:11–13

Having defeated the prophets of Baal on Mount Carmel, Elijah flees for his life to a cave on Mount Horeb. He had gone from one extreme to another – seeing the power of God and experiencing the elation of victory to feeling the depths of despair as he goes on the run from those who want to kill him. There, in a cave, when he is at his lowest point, God speaks to him, and shows him not just his power but also his presence. God tells Elijah to go and stand at the mouth of the cave so that he can be renewed and refreshed by being in God's presence. A mighty and powerful wind passed by, followed by an earthquake, then fire, but God was not in any of those things. Instead, it is in a gentle whisper that God comes close and speaks to Elijah.

Often, and particularly when we are struggling, we want God to shout things from the rooftops and write things in the sky; sometimes he's speaking so quietly and so gently we can miss it, because were waiting for the thunderbolt or lightning in the sky.

A few years ago, for various reasons I experienced a period where I felt a bit low. It coincided with starting a new job, and I was feeling a bit sorry for myself. What I told myself in that season of time was that I wasn't being taken seriously. It was something that was quite important to me, and the more I thought about it, the sorrier I felt for myself. One day, when I was indulging in an all-out pity party, my friend Toby phoned up out of the blue and said, 'Bill, I was praying for you and I got this word for you: I think God wants to tell you that he takes what you say and think really seriously.'

I don't know if you've ever felt like this, but I was feeling so sorry for myself that I didn't really want to hear it. I said, 'Thanks so much for that, bye,' and put the phone down. I was having too much fun feeling sorry for myself.

I got home that evening, and my middle son Jonah, who was seven at the time, had made me promise I would go and say goodnight to him. So, I went in as he was just going to bed. As I walked in, he sat up in his bed, pressed his index finger into my forehead, and said, 'Dad, there's a really good brain in there.' I stared at him – completely floored. It wasn't enough that God had tried to speak to me through my friend Toby, he had to speak to me through my seven-year-old son for it to get through.

The next day, without wanting to get too intense, I asked Jonah to talk me through why he said that; and to paraphrase, he said he just had a thought that came into his head out of nowhere, so he told me and went to sleep.

GOD ALSO THUNDERS

> The LORD thundered from heaven;
>   the voice of the Most High resounded.
> PSALM 18:13

Sometimes God speaks to us in a still small voice, so gently that we don't always recognise it, and some of us will hear this in our inner ear as a thought. However, others may well hear it as *an audible voice*. Just in the way that some will encounter the presence of God by just knowing – because we are *knowers* – or feeling, if we are *feelers*, when we encounter the voice of God through our sense of hearing, whether as an inner voice or an external audible voice, this indicates that we encounter God speaking to us as *hearers*.

The prophet Samuel is a great example of this – in 1 Samuel 3:1–11 we see him encounter the voice of God as a hearer three times – each time God calls his name 'Samuel, Samuel.' It's clear it is an audible voice of some kind – because he thinks Eli is calling him – but Eli himself isn't able to hear it.*

At other times the voice of God is audible to others; we read about God first speaking audibly to Jesus at his baptism and then to his closest friends during the transfiguration, both times with the same affirming words – 'This is my beloved son.' And the voice is heard by others there. Similarly at another point when Jesus is speaking in the temple, a voice came from heaven, and some in the crowd said it had thundered, and others said an angel had spoken. And at many points in the Gospels, the Old Testament, and also in the Book of Revelation, the voice of God is likened to thunder.**

'THE ONLY TIME YOU NEED TO WORRY IS WHEN I STOP TALKING'

Suddenly the operating theatre went very quiet. It was then that I remembered the anaesthetist's words before Nici underwent an emergency caesarean after a labour that had not gone well.

'The only time you need to worry is when I stop talking.'

The silence lasted what seemed like an age. It was the surgeon who punctured the silence.

'I can't stop her bleeding … Get him out of here.'
And with the surgeon's instruction, I suddenly found myself being politely bundled out of the operating theatre.

The good news was that our newborn baby son was breathing okay and was on his way up to the NICU (Neonatal Intensive Care Unit). The more worrying thing was Nici was quite obviously not in a good way at all.

I was ushered down the corridor and told to wait for a member of the operating theatre team to come and talk to me. A few minutes later

---

* Other examples of the voice of God being audible internally are perhaps when he speaks to the Old Testament prophets, such as in Ezekiel 2:2, 'I heard him speaking to me.'
** See for example Matthew 3:17; 17:5; John 12:29; Psalm 29:3; Revelation 14:2.

one of the nurses came out. 'The surgeon is having some problems stopping your wife bleeding. She has lost a lot of blood. They are working on her now and are doing all they can,' she said slowly.

As soon as the nurse had gone, I pulled out my phone and, notwithstanding the fact that it was 4am, frantically started messaging everyone I could think of, asking them to pray.

I felt a wave of fear begin to overwhelm me.

What if this was it? Was Nici going to die? How would I tell our boys? ... Surely, she would be okay ... Wouldn't she?

The surgeon's words echoed in my head, 'I can't stop her bleeding ... ' Over and over again.

There are times when we struggle to find the words to articulate all that we are feeling. 'Oh, God, please, please help,' was all I could summon up as I prayed desperately. 'Please, please don't let her die.'

My mind was moving at a thousand miles an hour now, in full disaster mode, the corridor empty and eerily quiet. I sat on the only chair, bent over, face in hands.

And then, out of nowhere,

'I'm here with you.'

I looked up to see who the kind man talking to me was. The corridor was empty.

And then the voice again, clearer than before, full of compassion and kindness:

'I'm here with you.'

My head was spinning – was I hallucinating under the stress of the situation? Hearing audible voices when I was sitting on my own in what was, and remains, one of the most terrifying moments of my life?

Or was it God? Speaking clearly to me in a reassuring voice in a moment of great need where my mind couldn't have processed a picture given to me in my mind's eye, or felt his presence, and, given the heightened emotional state I was in, a knowing would have passed me by.

And then, for a third time, fracturing my fear and calming my confusion,

'Bill, I'm here with you.'

It would be disingenuous to say that at that moment all my fear left me. My wife was still on the operating table, and the doctors were still fighting to stop the bleeding, but in that moment, in amidst the fear and uncertainty, I was clear of one thing. I was not alone. The creator of the universe had come close. God was there, in that corridor with me.

Thankfully the surgeons managed to stop Nici bleeding, but not before she had lost half of the blood in her body. She made a full recovery and that baby is now a healthy teenager.

I have often thought about the events of that night, about the kindness of God. When, literally, all my other senses were overloaded with emotion, God *spoke*. Not in my inner ear, where it might have been lost, but audibly.

While I have shared much of this story, this is the first time I have included hearing the audible voice of God. Not for fear of being misunderstood, but because it felt too precious, too intimate a moment between a Father and a son to share.

I have never heard the voice of God before or since, but this I know – it was what I needed when I most needed it.

---

practise

In your personal prayer time this week, whether you are out walking or in your own room, try using your voice. Choose an appropriate place and time, and try reading Scripture aloud, perhaps learning and reciting a psalm or a favourite passage, or perhaps speaking in tongues, or perhaps just speaking out your prayers.

---

learning to bear the weight of privilege

Do your best to present yourself to God as one approved, a worker who does not need to be ashamed and who correctly handles the word of truth.

2 TIMOTHY 2:15

'I don't understand – it's as if God has gone quiet,' I said, leaning over my cup of tea at the cafe next to the railway station.

Carl sat quietly for a few moments.

'Have I done something wrong?' I asked.

I could see Carl thinking, weighing up what to say. My mind was going into overdrive as I went over the past weeks and months – *was* there something I had done wrong?

Eventually, Carl spoke. 'Bill, maybe you just need to lower the ariel.'

'Lower the ariel? I'm not sure I follow.'

'Maybe it's not to do with anything you have done. Maybe this silence you are experiencing is because it's not so much that you want to receive a word – maybe you feel like you *need* one.'

Now it was my turn to pause. I knew immediately what Carl was saying. If I was honest, I had begun to feel it a few months before. People were beginning to look at me and see me as someone who could hear from God and share what I had received on any given occasion, and I was feeling a pressure to 'come up with the goods'. The second thing I had to admit to was a slow and dawning realisation that, as others began to notice in me a gift in the area of prophecy and words of knowledge, and that I was encountering the heart and voice of God, albeit in a very small way and with baby steps, I was quite enjoying the attention and recognition.

While perhaps not immediately obvious to anyone else, these things had begun to register internally, and I was feeling a tension between a real desire to share God's heart for people with them and this other slightly less altruistic motivation. It was the strange and uncomfortable feeling of being in a no man's land entirely of my own making.

One of the things I appreciated about Carl as a mentor was that he never expressed any hint of judgment, but rather took time to understand me and what I was wrestling with and was fully invested in my growth. It was always worth the train journey to visit him.

'Bill, sometimes, God appears to go quiet *because* he loves us. On the one hand whenever we open up the Bible and start reading, we are encountering God's voic. On the other he sometimes steps back, just a little, and while he doesn't appear to be saying anything, actually he's speaking really clearly.'

I was trying to take in what Carl was saying, although I was still a little unsure.

'At the end of the day, Bill, God isn't preparing you for ministry, he is preparing you for himself. In seasons like the one you are in, what he is saying is that he loves you too much to leave you alone – to leave you to your gifting. He wants to lead each of us to a place where he can continue to form us so that our character can carry the weight of the gifting.'

I knew he was right, but it didn't make it easier to hear.

'He takes as long as he knows it needs. He loves you far too much, he is too invested in you to be in a rush shaping you,' Carl replied to the next question I was about to ask. 'It took Michelangelo over two years of hard work, most of which was done in secret, to carve his statue of David out of the block of marble he began with. Some of the most breathtaking valleys were formed by glaciers moving slowly over hundreds of years.'

I was beginning to register what he was saying.

'Bill, the finest wines, the most delicious cheeses, are the ones that have been given time to mature. God wants to trust you with the most incredible and precious gift – the ability to encounter his heart for people and share it with them in a way that can have a profound and often life-changing impact on them. Hold onto that, engage with the process. Chase after deeper friendship with him not because of what he can tell you, but because, more than the gift, more than anything else, your heart longs for him. The gift isn't the prize – he is. And he is worth it.'

The more I thought about what Carl had said over the following weeks, the more it made sense. How easy it was, I thought, to become more interested in the gift than the giver at times.

I found myself reminded of an incident many years earlier. I had gone to stay with some dear friends who had three young children. With their parent's permission I had given each of them some money as a gift when I arrived, as a way of making up for missing their birthdays earlier that year. The children were all excited to be the recipients of, in their oldest sibling's words, 'actual real money'. It felt nice to be able to give something to them, if only as a reflection of my affection for each of the children.

One morning, a couple of days later, the oldest boy, who must have been about ten at the time, came up to me at breakfast and said, 'Can I have some more money?'

'Darling, Bill has already been very kind and given you some money,' said their father.

'But can't I have some more?' implored the child. I smiled slightly nervously, a little unsure of what to say.

My friend gently explained that as a good friend, I had given money to all of the children as a one-off gift to make up for the birthdays I had missed that year.

'But why can't I have some more? Wouldn't an even better friend give more?' asked his son, looking a bit confused.

'No – a good friend doesn't need to give anything. We're all just pleased he's here,' replied his father.

I didn't have children at the time but watching as the situation unfolded was a masterclass in parenting. But if I was being honest, at the time I felt a little hurt – it was as if the child in question was more interested in my money than he was my company. (As a parent now myself, I can see how it is understandable behaviour in a ten-year-old!)

The more I thought about that moment, the more I began to see how easy it can be to become like a child who just wants the money. It is easier than perhaps we like to recognise to fall into treating God like a benevolent giver of gifts, or worse still a slot machine, rather than the One who knows us, loves us and has a plan for our lives. What should be a friendship can, very subtly, become a transactional interaction, where, if we are not careful, we can inadvertently find ourselves carrying a sense of entitlement.

When that happens, and it can happen slowly over a number of years, this sense of entitlement hardens into an attitude which can, if left unchecked, begin to take hold. When it does, this will eventually have an adverse effect on our character.

I know from my own life how insidious and pernicious this can be, and writing a chapter about character feels very uncomfortable, as if to imply that in some way I think I have arrived, or that things like this are no longer an issue for me. Nothing could be further from the truth. I am painfully aware of my own shortcomings, of the battles I have had with my own poor attitudes and character flaws – sometimes glaring and sometimes subtle – and no doubt will continue to have as my own character continues to be formed.

In any kind of prophetic ministry, it is so important that the person who is communicating the heart of God for another can be trusted. We have to be able to trust that what they are sharing comes from a place of love for God and love for us, and is not clouded by, for example, a need to 'perform', or a need for recognition, or a sense of envy. We need to know we can trust the person themselves, that they have integrity, that they are of good character, and that they are authentic.*

This isn't supposed to be a burden, or an excuse for the less confident to disqualify ourselves. There will always be someone who is more gifted than us, but it doesn't mean we shouldn't still exercise our own gifts; far from it. One of the things I often remind myself of is the cast of characters that make up much of the Bible. Many were on their own character formation journeys, and some took longer to get there than others! We are all works in progress.

In many ways the story of Joseph illustrates much that I have said. It is worth taking some time to read the story again, even if you are familiar with it. It is a story of someone with an extraordinary gifting, someone who ultimately saves a nation, and someone who is shaped by a God whose relentless love for him means that he continues to be with him and work in him even when it seems that he is far off. It is a story I find myself coming back to again and again, and one that continues to captivate and challenge me.

At the beginning of Genesis 37 we find a complicated family scenario – Jacob and his one remaining wife, two servant girls or concubines and all their respective children. The family has been beset for years by deep-seated rivalries. Joseph is Jacob's favourite, the longed-for son of the much-loved wife who died when Joseph was around six. Now Joseph is a youth of seventeen, with ten older brothers, grown men in their twenties and thirties. They manage the family's considerable livestock and defend the family unit, but

---

* See for example Micah 3:5; Jeremiah 15:19.

are a formidable force, who have shown they are not afraid to use violence and have also flouted their father's authority. Reuben has slept with his father's concubine, and Simeon and Levi have made the family's position precarious with the wholesale slaughter of the men of the neighbouring community in revenge for the rape of their sister.

Against this background, Jacob sends Joseph to pasture the flocks with four of his brothers, the sons of the servant concubines, and puts Joseph in charge. Even though he's the younger brother, in Middle Eastern culture, the son of a wife would take precedence over the sons of servant girls. Joseph – perhaps intimidated by his brothers, determined to make his mark, and fulfilling his new role a little too conscientiously – brings a bad report of his brothers to his father. His father affirms his support and authority with the gift of a long-sleeved robe, and his brothers hate him; they can't speak a civil word to him.

It is in this precarious position that Joseph begins to experience God speaking to him. He tells his brothers about the dream, in which their sheaves of wheat bow down to his. They are furious. Even so, when Joseph has a second dream, he recounts that too; this time it includes his parents bowing down to him. This only adds fuel to the fire – the brothers hate him even more. His father, who as a younger man had also experienced God speaking to him through dreams,* rebukes him, perhaps partly to deflect the brothers' anger, but still he 'kept the matter in mind.'**

TO SHARE, OR TO KEEP THE MATTER IN MIND?

The question is: why does Joseph share his dreams – knowing it will upset his brothers – twice?

It is possible that God meant Joseph to share his dreams – it may have been such a strong, overpowering dream that Joseph felt compelled to share it, or even that God told him to share the dream,

* Genesis 28:10–22.
** Genesis 37:11.

even though he knew it was dangerous. We are later told, after all, that God had meant Joseph's trials for good.

We are perhaps more likely to see Joseph as someone who is a little arrogant, with a slightly brash adolescent lack of sensitivity and humility, lacking the *social* awareness to anticipate how others might respond to the dream and how offended they might feel. Or we might see Joseph as lacking *self*-awareness: he'd grown up without a mother and was perhaps unaware of his own inner need for affirmation, his secret desire for respect and a secure position within the family.

Or, it's possible Joseph may have made a tactical decision. Joseph was young, being groomed for a position of leadership over a formidable group. His father sees leadership qualities in him, while some of his older brothers had forfeited their right to precedence. But his position is precarious, and in a community ruled by physical strength he needs to find a way to make his mark, to establish his position. Divine endorsement or mandate is just what he needs.

Whichever way you read it – as a deliberate and courageous act of obedience, as a desperate attempt to establish authority, or as a lack of social and self-awareness pointing to a lack of humility, there is a lot to learn from this story.

ULTERIOR MOTIVES?

There are many examples of false prophets in the Bible, and contemporary examples of people who have been attracted to the ministry of the Spirit, prophecy and healing included, for the wrong reasons. While on the face of it their hunger to operate in these things can be noteworthy or even initially inspiring, it can also be something of a smokescreen for an agenda which has much less to do with having a desire for people to encounter the love, goodness, kindness and power of God, and more to do with someone's own desire for attention or personal gain.

Simon the Sorcerer in Acts 8:9–24 is an example of this. He has operated in some form of supernatural gifting and has seen the impact of the ministry of the Spirit on those who have been baptised in it, so much so that he offers money to receive the ability to see people he prays for receive the Holy Spirit.

While this is a more obvious example of someone whose character as a young believer still needed a lot of work, we need to be aware in ourselves of the times when we might use other means to ingratiate ourselves to people for often well-meaning but ultimately ulterior motives.

The majority of the people that I have encountered over the years have been well-meaning, well-intentioned people who long to see God reveal himself, and often their chief concern is a worry that they might be asking for a spiritual gift for the wrong reason.

If you are someone who worries you might be asking for the wrong reason, or with the wrong motivation, my own experience is that you probably don't need to worry – the fact that you are aware that this could be an issue almost always means that it isn't. But it is something to reflect on and bear in mind.

A WORK IN PROGRESS

Joseph was seventeen. When I think back to some of the things I said and did at his age, I have to wonder what I was thinking at the time. We can only speculate, but I sometimes wonder if Joseph has not yet learned what it means to be a friend of God – to carry the secrets that have been shared with him. Maybe he hasn't yet learned what the impact of sharing a word can be. And maybe he hasn't the maturity to recognise the danger of using God's word for our own purposes.

What I find so encouraging about this initial introduction to Joseph is that while he may have been inexperienced and flawed, God still spoke to him. God didn't wait until he was mature and experienced before he began to speak to him, because, as we have already seen, God speaks to us because he loves us, because he wants us to know his heart. It is always relational.

It's interesting to track the trajectory of Joseph's journey, to see how from a brash and insensitive teenager, a true leader is slowly formed. Narrowly escaping murder at his brothers' hands, he was sold into slavery to some travelling Midianite merchants for twenty shekels. It is hard to imagine the trauma he experienced walking alongside the merchant's convoy, wondering how he found himself there, a slave heading towards a foreign land. Perhaps he began to ask himself how he might have avoided stirring up such resentment and hatred in his brothers, how he might have handled his father's favour more wisely. Much like Michelangelo, God is quietly chipping away at the marble in Joseph's life.

When the convoy arrived in Egypt he is sold again, this time to Potiphar who was one of Pharaoh's officials. He is alone, far from home in a foreign land, probably afraid. His doting father is at home grieving his apparent death at the hand of wild animals, an elaborate hoax by his siblings to cover up their actions. The picture could hardly be bleaker. Nevertheless, we are told, he prospers. God had not forgotten him. Whatever he turns his hand to succeeds.*

It is not long before Potiphar recognises that there is something special about this young slave, and promotes him to his attendant, putting him in charge of everything he owns. I wonder if Joseph began to become overconfident in his own ability, with this new favour he has been shown, the trust his master has placed in him, and his rank in the household. His response to Potiphar's wife's increasingly brazen sexual advances, 'No one is greater in this house than I am,' hints, at least to a degree, of that overconfidence that we saw earlier.

While Joseph showed integrity and ran from these unwanted advances, the spurned mistress of the house turned the tables on him and accused him of wanting to 'make sport of me.'**

* Genesis 39:2–3.
** Genesis 39:17.

Once again Joseph finds himself alone, this time in prison. And yet, even there, we are told, 'the LORD was with him; he showed him kindness and granted him favour in the eyes of the prison warden.'*

Favour followed Joseph, the administrative gifts that he had used so effectively for Potiphar were now being utilised in captivity. More than that, while as a younger man God had spoken to him in dreams, Pharaoh's chief cupbearer and baker, who had both offended their master and found themselves in prison, tell Joseph about the dreams they have both had. With God's help, Joseph interpreted their dreams and then watched as both were fulfilled three days later, just as the dreams he had interpreted foretold.

Despite his promise to tell Pharaoh about Joseph's predicament and intercede on his behalf, upon release and restoration to his role, the chief cupbearer forgets Joseph.

We do not know why the chief cupbearer forgets – perhaps it served to confirm Joseph's gift as an interpreter of dreams, but the time had not yet come for him to help Pharaoh. My own supposition is that God used that time to continue to carve Joseph's character and to chip away at any sense of entitlement, or reliance he might have developed on his gifting, and the way he had been able to utilise it to turn situations round for his advantage.

And so Joseph remains in his dungeon. Hope of rescue fading as each day passes. More time to let go of his self-reliance and continue his journey to become fully reliant on the God who had never forgotten him, nor ceased to be at work in his life. More time to look back and think.

'It is just so tough,' he said, only half-looking at me.

I kept quiet and left space for him to finish.

'It's the time you have, the hours of it, just to think, "How did I end up here?"' He paused and offered a wry, self-aware smile. 'Apart from the armed robbery bit ... '

* Genesis 39:21.

We were sitting in the chapel in one of England's more notorious prisons sipping tea. In some ways it could have been like so many of the pastoral conversations I have had over the years – often over a cup of tea, listening as the person sitting in front of me shared their story, and searched for answers. The only difference being that the man I was spending time with was serving a ten-year stretch for holding up a post office with a sawn-off shotgun, and a very large prison guard stood at a respectful distance, keeping a watchful eye on proceedings.

'You just go over and over everything in your head … it's not just that I'm forgotten in here, and that life goes on for those on the outside but having the time to think about what I did, and why I did it,' he paused briefly, considering what he said next for a moment. 'And what kind of a man I've become. That's the worst bit.'

Joseph was innocent. And while we don't know many details – what kind of prison Joseph was in, the conditions, what his thoughts were, as these kinds of details are rarely given in Old Testament literature – it wouldn't be unreasonable to speculate that he would have spent a lot of time in self-reflection. And there was plenty of time: from being sold as a slave by his brothers, to finally being released from prison by Pharoah, it was around thirteen years. Michelangelo's raw marble slab, so to speak, was slowly but surely being carved away, and the figure of David – or Joseph, the leader and saviour of a nation – was beginning to take shape. God, always the master artist, is never in a rush. Joseph was too precious for that. And so are you and I.

It may be that you are reading this, and you find yourself in your own prison. Like Joseph, you have deployed all the means you have at your disposal – your gifts, your guile, your relational capital with someone – to facilitate your own deliverance, and yet you still wait, hope fading by the day.

If that is you – hold on: God is closer than you think. He is at work in your life. Allow him to use this time to bring hidden things – the secret attitudes, the misplaced confidences or ill-conceived plans into the light. Engage in the struggle, allow him to use your experience to shape you.

The Joseph we encounter after his eventual release from prison two years later, who interprets Pharaoh's dreams and is subsequently promoted to be second only to the king in Egypt, is a very different man from the teenager we first encounter.

He does indeed witness the fulfilment of his two dreams – one of his brothers bowing down before him, the other of his aged parents doing the same. He has been so formed by God through all that he has experienced that he can say to his brothers, when he eventually reveals himself to them:

> 'And now, do not be distressed and do not be angry with yourselves for selling me here, because it was to save lives that God sent me ahead of you.'
>
> GENESIS 45:5

Nothing of Joseph's life and experience – of privilege, betrayal, slavery, promotion, imprisonment or despair – was wasted by God. All the while, whether he was out of his depth or overconfident and brash, that seventeen-year-old was being shaped and formed into a leader. He became the second most powerful man in the most advanced and sophisticated nation on the earth at the time. And when he did, he had the character to carry the weight of the gift and call that was on his life. Not just to save his family but deliver a nation from starvation.

THE WEIGHT OF PRIVILEGE

When Queen Elizabeth II was crowned Queen on 2nd June 1953, she wore two crowns for the occasion: she wore the diamond encrusted Imperial State Crown on the way into the ceremony, and on her coronation the twenty-two carat gold St Edward's Crown, which weighs over two kilogrammes. It was so heavy that she had to practise wearing it before her coronation so that she was strong enough to carry its weight.

The same is true for us – God will use any situation he can to strengthen us so that we are able to carry the gift that he has given us. That way, when we do encounter his voice, we have the character to carry the weight of that privilege. Not because we need a word from him, not in order to strengthen our standing in other people's eyes, not to ingratiate ourselves with others, not because we enjoy the attention or crave recognition, but because friendship with him is the great longing in our hearts, and he loves to share his heart with his friends.

A number of years ago I was working at a church conference and one of the speakers I looked after was someone that I had respected for many years as someone who had a profound gifting in the prophetic. The more time I spent with her and her husband, who I had known vaguely for a number of years, the more I saw how their deep friendship with God had shaped their prophetic ministry.

Eventually, at the end of the conference, as we were saying our goodbyes, I asked them if they would pray for me to grow in the gift of prophecy that they carried.

'But of course, dear Bill!' they exclaimed. 'We must!'

I can't recall everything that they prayed that afternoon, but I do remember two things: the first was that God would do whatever it took to draw me after him, and the second was that I would allow God to speak to me and use me in that way, particularly when it felt unusual and uncomfortable.

When they had finished praying, we said our goodbyes and I waited with anticipation to see what might begin to happen as a result of their prayers.

What I did not expect was a period where I began to become aware of subtle attitudes that I had hitherto not been aware of. While there was no glaring major character flaw, it was uncomfortable and at times painful to process and deal with them.

'Bill, it seems from what you're saying that God is shaping your character,' said my friend Piers as we walked across Wandsworth Common to a cafe one autumn afternoon a few months later. 'That's a good thing!'

'It doesn't feel that great,' I replied.

'When you asked that couple to pray for you to grow in the prophetic you were essentially inviting discomfort … there is no meaningful growth without it. God is too committed to you to give you a greater gifting without working in you so that you don't get in the way of it. Didn't they say that God was going to use you when it felt unusual and uncomfortable?'

I didn't respond.

'Embrace it and watch what happens.'

I was at work a few days later, and one of my work colleagues who had been particularly helpful with some admin I had been struggling with kept coming to mind. I just could not get her out of my mind. After my experience on the Wandsworth roundabout a year or so earlier, and seeing the impact that one phone call and the subsequent coffee had had on Simon, I had continued to learn and lean into those nudges.

'Lord, what's going on? What are you wanting to say?' I asked. Almost immediately I was reminded of a book that I had read earlier that year that had had a real impact on me, and then, what I can only describe as a gentle whisper spoke quietly in my inner ear, 'Give her a copy of that book.'

To be honest it felt a bit of an unusual thing to do, and I wasn't sure how I was going to explain it to her, but I went to the church bookshop and bought the last remaining copy, wrote a quick note on a postcard and headed back to the office to see if my colleague was at her desk.

She looked up as I walked towards her, 'Hi,' I said somewhat awkwardly. 'You came to mind earlier, and I was thinking how grateful I was for your help recently.'

I could tell she was wondering where the conversation was going. It was beginning to feel a little uncomfortable. I smiled in an attempt to lighten the mood.

'Anyway, I read this book earlier on in the year and I thought you might like it, by way of a thank you for all your help.'

'Er … thanks, Bill,' she replied, taking the book.

'No worries, thanks again, and I hope you enjoy it.'

I had all but forgotten the entire incident until, just over two years ago, and nearly three and a half years after it took place, by which time we had both left the church we had both been working for, she came to speak one Sunday morning at our church in Guildford.

'Bill, do you remember that book you gave me as a thank you after I had helped you with some admin?'

I thought for a moment. 'Yes, how did you find it?' I asked.

'To be honest I got home and put it on my shelf and forgot about it until earlier on this year.'

'Oh, okay,' I said. 'I had received prayer that I would grow in the prophetic, and actually what had happened was that God started working on me instead! I'm so sorry if I got it wrong with the book.'

'No, you don't understand … I still don't know why you bought it for me,' she said. 'But thank you. So much,' she paused for a moment, taking a deep breath.

'That book saved my life.'

Like Joseph, and so many of the others we read about in the Bible, and throughout church history, we are all works in progress. Wherever we are in our journey with him, God's invitation is to allow him to shape our character so that we can carry the gift he wants to grow in us.

If we are willing to embrace this shaping, God will work in us in such a way that he will come to be the great longing in our hearts. More than that, as we walk with him, he will continue to shape us into living works of art that he will use to share his presence, his goodness and his love to those we meet.

practise

○ Think back to a time a friend shared a secret with you. How did that impact your relationship? Why do you think God might share secrets with you?

○ Looking back on your own life, have there been times when God has taught you something through a difficult or challenging time? What was it? How has this shaped you?

pray, practise, and persevere

Now faith is confidence in what we hope for and assurance about what we do not see.

HEBREWS 11:1

ON GETTING IT WRONG

I have really wrestled with sharing my stories in this book. I long to encourage, but would never want anyone to think, 'Wow, that's amazing, but I could never do that.' Inevitably when we share our stories, we tell our Greatest Hits. We tell the stories of the times when it went really, really well, and we're not so forthcoming about the times when it was a total disaster.

So, for that reason, and for the sake of full disclosure, I want to share a time when it went exceptionally badly.

It was in a church meeting, and someone caught my eye. As I've said before, I've learned to pay attention when someone catches my eye more than once or twice in a meeting or gathering. In those situations, I begin to ask, 'Lord, do you have something to say to this person?'

It's either the person at the back who doesn't want to be there that I'm really interested in, or the one who catches my eye for no apparent reason. As I said, I was at a church meeting, and this person caught my eye, and I just began to get a sense of what I thought God wanted to say to them, and I said, 'Lord, please give me your heart for this person,' and it often starts with a heart for them and then that often develops into something clearer, much like an old polaroid photograph. It can be easy to take the initial revelation and run with that, rather than giving God the time to slowly reveal the details. The more time in the light, the more colour, texture and detail God shows us..

So, I went up to this person, and I started to share, and the person started to react to what I was saying, so I thought, 'Great, this is good.' I thought that what I had said had registered a reaction with them. We often go off visual clues that are not about reading a person but just looking for a response. So, in the moment I thought, 'Right, they seem to be responding, so I'll keep going.'

At this point the person started to cry a bit more, and I thought, 'Wow, I'm on a roll here,' so I kept going. Eventually I finished what I had been sharing and offered to pray for them. The person, who looked somewhat shellshocked by this point, said, 'I'd rather you didn't, if you don't mind,' and smiled awkwardly and walked away quite quickly.

It was as the person walked off that it dawned on me that, on reflection, it hadn't gone quite as well as I thought it had been going. I happened to be with my friend Alex at the time, who looked at me and said, 'Well, Bill, that was interesting.'

The euphemism 'interesting' in that culture was a very polite way of saying that something really hadn't gone well. At all. I knew he was right. I was starting to have one of those 'What. Were. You. Thinking?' moments.

'I think it started well, then went into a tailspin and crash-landed.'

'Yes, it did,' said Alex. 'Bill, what happened was that when she started to cry, you responded to that by charging in like a bull in a china shop. You didn't actually check in with her, or ask about her response, you just kept going. You crashed through all of her barriers because you thought you were onto something and were just going to go for it.'

As we talked about it over a cup of tea, I began to see what had happened. The initial bit that I'd shared had been right, and she had started to cry, not because she was moved or touched by God, but because she was really uncomfortable – shocked and caught unawares. In the moment, because I hadn't thought to pause and ask her if she was okay, if everything was okay, I had misunderstood and misjudged what was happening in that moment, and because of that, I kept going.

If I'd explained what was happening to her before I had even shared anything at all, rather than assuming she was familiar with the prophetic, and asked if she would like to hear what I thought God might be saying, she might have felt she could have either said yes, she would like to hear it, or that she wouldn't. I hadn't given her that opportunity.

If I had stopped after what I felt God had said initially, the core of which was good, the situation might have been able to be redeemed; but, because I just kept going, because in all honesty in that moment it had become more about me than the other person, it became something that didn't have life in it, that made her feel caught in a situation she didn't fully understand or know how to get out of. The consequence was that in my eagerness to share, and frankly because my attitude of thinking I was on a bit of a roll was so appalling, the situation had rapidly gone downhill.

I learned a lot from that experience, and I'm not proud of it.

SHARING WELL

In this chapter we're going to look at some practicalities and pitfalls of operating in the prophetic.

I've learned, often the hard way, that how we communicate what God shares with us when we encounter his presence and his heart for someone really can make a huge difference in someone's life, if it is done well. As I said in the last chapter, prophecy is a gift that we can all grow in if we take the time to practise.

Practising, and really understanding and knowing some of the practicalities about what, how and when to share something will really amplify this amazing gift and enable you to grow in it and take it to the next level. This is a biblical principle that Jesus outlined in the parable of the talents.* Whatever the level of our initial gifting might be, if we invest in it, God will give us more.

Paul writes,

We have different gifts, according to the grace given to each of us. If your gift is prophesying, then prophesy in accordance with your faith.
ROMANS 12:6

What Paul is doing is recognising right at the beginning, and we know this from the parable of the talents, that not everybody is given an equal measure of gifting at the start. That doesn't mean that we can't get better. God decides how much grace he gives us, if any, to start with, and the extent to which we're prepared to step out and practise, we will grow. And the extent to which we're prepared to learn, will be the extent to which we grow.

Some days we will be full of faith and feel we could share a word from God with everybody, and there are days, speaking for myself, where I just don't feel like I've got it in the tank. It's not that I don't have faith; I feel like I have enough faith for me, but not much for anybody else. And it's okay to acknowledge that; 'Faith is confidence in what we hope for and assurance about what we do not see,'** but it's also being realistic both about who God is but also about where we're at, at any given time.

JUST APOLOGISE

The first lesson I've learned is that if I ever make a mistake – cross a line, go over a boundary, or make someone feel unsafe, get it wrong

* Matthew 25:14–30.
** Hebrews 11:1.

in a thousand different ways – the only way to rescue that situation is to put my hand up and say, 'I just messed up; I am really sorry.'

Don't make excuses, just own it. Own your mistakes. Learn from them. In my experience, people are far more forgiving if we are prepared to apologise than if we just make some excuse which deep down both parties know is a face-saving exercise, or worse still, a veiled criticism of them.

In the example I shared above, the reality was that the situation was in my hands; it was within my power to stop at any point, but I didn't. And so, I needed to own that. And apologise. Fortunately, Alex knew her, and I had the chance to apologise.

FOR PRAYER, OR TO SHARE?

The next thing I learned from that situation was that if God starts to speak to you about someone, almost the first question to ask is, 'Lord, is this for me to know and pray about, or is this for me to share?' Often, we assume it is for us to share and keep going without actually having got an answer one way or the other. But sometimes the Lord is confiding in us, revealing his secrets. God told Daniel to 'seal up the vision, for it concerns the distant future', and to 'roll up and seal the words of the scroll until the time of the end'. And Paul was unable to speak of parts of his vision on the road to Damascus because he 'heard inexpressible things, things that no one is permitted to tell'.*

I try to make this my first prayer, when I begin to encounter God speaking to me about someone else – immediately after 'Is this you, Lord?' I will ask, 'Lord, is this for me to know and pray about, or for me to share?'

Over the years I have found that often God is giving me an insight so that I can pray for the person, and I need to wait for an opportune moment to share with them once I sense that it is right to do so. Sometimes God has given you something that you need to hold onto, and the more you hold onto it the more weight and depth and colour

---

* Psalm 25:14; Amos 3:7; Daniel 8:26; 12:4; 2 Corinthians 12:4.

and detail it gains, so that at the right moment when it is ready to share, the impact of that on the person's life is far more significant.

By all means share what the Lord has given you, if you feel he's given you a clear green light to share. But don't assume. First stop and reflect, pray, and ask yourself in this moment, 'Is this something that is going to encourage if I share it now? Or could it be even more encouraging if I held onto it?'

KEEPING CONFIDENCES

> *Surely the Sovereign LORD does nothing*
> *without revealing his plan*
> *to his servants the prophets.*
> AMOS 3:7

God wants to reveal his heart to his friends; but we have to act like his friends, and like close confidants. If you told me something confidential, and then I went and told four other people, and you found out, the probability is that you are not going to tell me anything confidential anytime soon, because I have broken your trust. In the same way, when the Lord trusts us with things that are on his heart, if we end up using them for gossip, or if we mishandle them, in his kindness he will lead us back to a place where he can trust us again, even if that means he holds his voice back for a time.

I remember once having this knowing about someone. I wasn't really sure what to do about it or how to use this revelation, and ended up blurting it out to some of the people I was with when that person came up in conversation. As soon as I had opened my mouth, I knew that I should not have. I sensed the Lord gently challenge me, '*I shared this with you to deepen your understanding and compassion for that person, not so that you could weaponise it and share it.*' I've learned that rather than getting frustrated with people in those situations, actually it's best to turn it into a prayer for that person.

JUST BE YOURSELF

Another thing I learned when I made a mess of things with my friend Alex watching on, was that I had become a little arrogant and thought that I was on a bit of a roll – at times like this, we can so easily move into performance mode, where our focus is more on ourselves and how we are doing in that moment than it is on God or the other person. My friend Alex put it really well as we talked about what had happened. 'Bill,' he said. 'You are already awesome. You don't need to try to be more awesome. You don't need to perform. Just be you. Know that you're loved, know that God speaks to you, and let that be enough.'

WITH REVERENCE

> The LORD confides in those who fear him;
> he makes his covenant known to them.
> PSALM 25:14

The Lord shares his heart with those who approach him with reverence. What that means is that we take what he says seriously enough not to mess around with it or with people. Prophecy isn't a game, it's not a way of trying to impress somebody and it's not a toy; it is an incredible privilege to share heart to heart with somebody what you feel, and sense what God might want to say to that person. In my own experience, when I have gone through seasons where my character has been a bit left behind in the excitement – perhaps I've lacked humility, or I've got a little bit cocky and overconfident – I find the Lord speaks to me less because I'm not approaching him with awe and reverence. I'm not taking seriously the incredible privilege of what he's shared with me. I've mishandled it. And it's not that he's punishing me, it's because he loves me and he loves the people that I am wanting to encourage.

GOD'S WORD AND CHARACTER

Another question to ask is: is what you sense God to be saying consistent with his word in Scripture? Some words are clearly consistent with the Bible, and some things are clearly not biblical, and so the answer should be straightforward. But there's also an ocean of grey in the middle, where there's seemingly nothing said directly in the Bible about what you're sensing God might be saying. In these cases, the filter to put the word through is to ask yourself some questions like this:

- Does it reflect the heart and the nature of Jesus as revealed in the Bible?
- Does it reflect the sort of thing Jesus might, or would, say, even if it's not specifically referred to in the Bible?
- Is it going to lead this person into a place where they encounter the heart of the Father?
- And even if it is based on Scripture, it's also always incredibly important to ask yourself if the word is edifying and encouraging in the context you share it.

If you are still not sure, find someone who is more experienced, seasoned prophetically or pastorally, or both, and ask them for their input.

WHEN TO FLUSH

There may also be times when you know that what someone shares with you is just wrong. It's not so much that it doesn't resonate, but that they are either unintentionally wrong, or on very rare occasions, just ill-intentioned. If that is the case, flush them, so to speak! Get rid of them.

One of my friends was at an event and someone came up and said 'I feel like I've got a word for you,' and it was just the most discouraging thing this person had heard for weeks. He asked me afterwards what he should do. I asked him, 'Well, how are you feeling?'

His reply was that he was feeling really discouraged. 'It's thrown me,' he said.

'Right,' I said. 'Flush it!'

If you have the confidence and the courage, I really want to encourage you to get good at giving honest feedback. The person who shared a word like the one I have described will not get better if they don't know. The second thing is that if you don't, you will end up leaving with a bad taste in your mouth that you could have done something about. Think about how you would want to receive constructive feedback, and do it in as generous, honest and encouraging a way as you can.

I've already given you an example of this (the word about being tired). I wanted to honour the person, so I told them the truth. And it wasn't particularly what they wanted to hear, and it's not because I thought I was better than them, but it's because I am invested in their success, that I tell them the truth. I want to invest in that person's growth. I want to invest in them getting even better at what they're chasing after – which means you have to give them feedback.

People in church ministering in the gifts of the Spirit should not be immune from feedback. One might argue that they need it more than most, because the stakes are even higher. It's because we love people and we want to honour what God is doing in them, and we want to honour their heart, and we want to honour the journey they're on, that we tell them. If I gave a rubbish sermon, I hope someone would say, 'How do you think that went?' and if I was honest I would say, 'Well, I think that bit went well but I'm not sure about that bit. What did you think?' and then the person would tell me.

In your work, if you're responsible for someone, I'm assuming you give them feedback; if someone is your boss at some point, they'll give you feedback. And I don't know whether they give good or bad feedback, but let's determine to do the same for the people around us.

WHEN OTHERS ASK FOR DIRECTION

The more we grow as friends of God and those who hear his voice, the more we may find others coming to us and essentially asking us for a word from God for them. This usually comes from a place of real longing for direction or wisdom from God.

I will always tell those people that I will be praying for them, but often also ask, 'Why would God talk to me about you when he could talk to you about you?' Sometimes they reply, 'Oh, but you're better at hearing God than me!' This is very humbling, but it is at this point that I will remind them that it's not necessarily that I'm better at hearing God than them at all, it's just that I've just got slightly more confidence in terms of sharing it.

WHAT IS IT THAT THE LORD WANTS TO REVEAL ABOUT HIMSELF?

When I sense the Lord starting to speak to me about somebody, or about a situation, the question that runs through my mind – and this is a good framework – is 'What is the Lord saying?' My second question is often 'What does he want to reveal about himself?' I've noticed that often it seems like when we share something prophetically it might appear to be information about the other person; but my observation is that God is always wanting to reveal himself to people. More than his plans, he wants people to know his nature. It may be to encourage someone that he is there with them in the situation they are worried about, or even more simply that he cares, he knows them and he sees them.

FROM THE RECEIVING END

We are all unique, and we all respond to prophetic words differently. My observation over the years has been that generally speaking, people fall into three categories. I have found it helpful to recognise these categories so that I have a better understanding of what might be going on, and also so that I can follow up appropriately where possible with people afterwards.

The first category are people who respond by thinking, in essence, 'This is my moment, is everybody listening?' For these people a prophetic word is a particularly big thing. They will often give the word lots of meaning because it aligns with what they want people to think about them, what they want to do, or just because in their minds it validates them. They will typically be looking for people to acknowledge what is going on in that moment. There is nothing inherently wrong with this response, but it is worth being aware of, as they will often come back and ask for clarification, and there have been occasions where what has been shared has taken on a whole new life and level of its own, so reminding them what you actually shared is helpful for them.

The second type of person is someone whose response is somewhat akin to a rabbit in the headlights. Their adrenaline starts to fire, their stress hormone starts to kick in, and they sometimes won't hear the first things that you say to them because they are slightly overwhelmed, slightly shocked, and not ready for it. Which is why it's really helpful if you say to someone, on a one-to-one basis, 'I feel like God might have something to say to you; would you like to hear it?' because when you do that, you're giving them time to get through that initial 'ahhh', or 'help!' or 'run away' moment. It is important with people who respond like this to give them time to calm down, and to begin to process what is happening, to speak slowly and clearly and keep checking in with them that they are okay, particularly as they can sometimes initially have an emotional response which is more a reaction to what is happening than it is to what you might be sharing, as was the case with the person in the story I shared earlier in the chapter. Once they have overcome their initial response it is good practice to ask them if they are okay and if they want you to share the word you have for them. If they respond, 'actually I'd rather you didn't,' that's alright. In that exchange your job is to offer the option of a prophetic word to the person. They have the right to say whether they want it or not. If they say no, you've done your job; leave it at that.

The third type of person is somebody who is by nature more reflective – they want to hear it, hold it lightly and ponder it. I would probably fall into that category. I just like to go away and think about things. I've noticed that often my initial reaction is a measured one, because I just want to go home, and I want to think about it, and I want to think how and whether it fits and what God is saying.

The best way to understand what is going on with someone is to ask! 'What's going on? How are you feeling? Just talk to me about what's going on right now.' Because when you allow somebody to talk about it, they can process their emotions appropriately, or begin to. And with that in mind, personally, maybe it's because I struggle to concentrate for very long at one time, I find the shorter the better. So, when you have a word for somebody, unless you're either super confident or really good, keep it postcard length.

People will thank you for a postcard; you don't need to write them a letter. It's better to leave people wanting more, than struggling to remember what you just said. Generally speaking, I think, 'God, what is the one thing you want this person to know about you?'

Think about how, if you were on the receiving end of what the person is saying, you would want to receive it? Of course, as I've already said, we all respond differently; but how would you want to receive this? You would want to be honoured, you would want to be not pushed into a corner, you would want to be allowed to process it in your own way, whichever category of response you fall into. So, think about sharing it in the way that you'd like to receive it.

OPEN WITH A QUESTION

You will hopefully have noticed that in many of the stories I have shared in this book I have started by asking questions. I think it's a good practice to ask questions rather than make statements, at least initially. A good example is, 'I feel like God has something he wants to say to you; would you like to hear it?' Open with a question. It gives the person a way out; and it actually also gives you a way out. If you suddenly feel you're not quite sure what you're doing, ask questions: would you like to carry on? Would you like to take a break? Is this making sense? It's good to check in with the person, which I didn't do in the story at the beginning, and the question that I often ask is, 'Is this making sense to you?' Always give people an out, because we want to respect their dignity, and we want to respect the fact that this isn't about us, it's about them.

KEEP IT SIMPLE

I think the more that we can use accessible and easy to understand language the better. Keep it simple. It can be very easy over time to learn and begin to use all kinds of religious jargon, and even easier to assume that the person you are talking to understands what you mean! Something doesn't become more spiritual if you use a spiritual word; you're just using a 'spiritual' word.

I had an experience of this recently. We have open sessions at our church where we encourage people to seek God and if they think or feel that he gives them something they could share with the whole church community to come and let me know, and we will work out together what it might mean, and how and when during the service the person might share it. I always caveat these times by saying that I can't guarantee that we will be able to share everything, and that if we don't get someone up to share it doesn't mean we don't believe they have encountered God's voice, but that we can't work out how to share it, or whether that particular service is the right moment. Someone came to the front and tapped me on the shoulder and said they thought that they had a word to share.

'Great!' I said. 'What is it?' She started to explain it to me and asked if it made sense.

'I hope you don't mind me saying this,' I replied, 'but I understand every single word you've used in English, and I have no idea what you're talking about. I know it's good because I can see the heart behind it, but I'm wondering if there is a way of saying this in

English?' I said it with a smile on my face, and she laughed. She had a quick think, rephrased it and when she shared it the service went to a whole new level as we worshipped in response.

John Wimber once said that 'Spiritual gifts are tools, not trophies.' They are tools – part of the toolkit that God has given us to make him known. In my experience, the best way to make him known is to keep it simple. Spiritual gifts, including prophecy, are tools; they're there to help us help people encounter Jesus.

I have a friend called Roger who talks about what he called 'Birnam' words – words that are so general and non-specific that they could apply to anyone or anything at any time. He would say that they are the equivalent of Christian fortune cookies, words that Macbeth might say are 'full of sound and fury, signifying nothing.'*

WAIT AND SEE

Often the prophetic can begin with something like that. Many years ago, I sensed God was saying something to a group of significant leaders who were meeting over a couple of days. I was so excited – I called my friend Mark and shared it with him. He listened carefully and then said to me, 'Bill, I think it's great. I'm just not sure what it means, other than it could be anything to anyone. It doesn't sound finished to me.'

I went quiet, and I suspect he could tell I felt somewhat crestfallen and confused.

'Bill, there's definitely something there, but I think that if you keep pressing in and asking God, he will give you more and make it clearer. Don't overthink it, just mull over it for a day or so. Think about it like a stew – the best ones are when the meat is allowed to settle and cook in its own juices – that's when the flavour and texture really comes out. Have the courage to allow God to take you to a deeper place with him. Wait and see what else he might want to say.'

* William Shakespeare, *Macbeth*, Act 5, Scene 5. Birnam is the name of the wood that features in a prophecy about the end of Macbeth's reign.

It was, as it turned out, extraordinarily helpful and encouraging advice. As I went away and tried not to overthink it, God began to speak more clearly. The voice of the Lord really was like the sound of many rushing waters.* The more I let what I had initially received settle, the more detail and insight I received. When I did send what I had received to the gathering of leaders, the feedback was that it had had a significant impact and confirmed much of what had been shared. Mark had taught me a valuable lesson, and one that I have lived by ever since. Have the courage and faith to wait and let God lead you deeper in him and where he has greater revelation for you.

There will be times, when what we share with someone doesn't resonate with them, no matter what questions we ask, how we frame it, the language we use or how long or short it is. Often this will have nothing to do with you at all, but rather a reflection of the place or time in their life that the person you are sharing with finds themself. Tempting as it can be, I have learned not to take it personally, remembering that the role of someone who has received a prophetic word is, to use an analogy, to deliver the mail, not kick the door down and stand over the person as you force them to read the post!

Finally, there will also be times when someone with the greatest of intentions might offer you a prophetic word. It could be that what they say reflects the nature and person of Jesus, is rooted in biblical truth and is so encouraging that God begins to draw you closer to himself.

There may, on occasion, be times when what is shared with you doesn't resonate initially at all. You might have to work out if this is something you're going to file, much like Mary did when the shepherds arrived to visit the newly born Jesus. Scripture says that 'Mary treasured up all these things and pondered them in her heart.'** If this is the case, file them and reflect on them and wait to see what God does.

* Ezekiel 43:2; Revelation 19:6.
** Luke 2:19.

As this chapter comes to a close, I want to encourage you. If you have read this far it is because you want to grow in the prophetic. Chase after it. It has been one of the great privileges of my life really, to see how something that I was maybe fifty or sixty per cent confident about sharing has impacted and changed someone's life. It's not because I'm brilliant at this; it is because I gave it a go. I chased after it, I took a risk, my heart leaping out of my mouth; I've got it wrong lots of times, but equally I've had the privilege of seeing what God does when we get up, dust ourselves off and have another go.

In order to chase after it, find people who are moving in this, ideally someone who's a little bit further on, and hang out with them, watch what they do, ask them questions and practise with them.

Finally, always remember that love is the key. If you love God, and you love the person, or you get God's heart for the person, and the message is loving, encouraging, reflects the character of Jesus as revealed in the Bible, is led by questions, and is short and non-religious, it will be a blessing.

---

practise

Has there ever been a time when a word someone shared with you didn't sit well with you? Why was that? What did you learn from that, in particular about giving good feedback?

---

strengthening what remains

challenging words

Those whom I love I rebuke and discipline. So be earnest and repent. Here I am! I stand at the door and knock. If anyone hears my voice and opens the door, I will come in and eat with that person, and they with me.

REVELATION 3:19–20

LET LOVE BE YOUR CURRENCY

I confess to being something of a people pleaser by nature. I love people, and frankly I quite like it when they love me back. So, when one day I had something of a knowing, a divine intuition, about someone I worked with that involved something they were doing in their private life, something that their best self would not have been proud of, I confess I ignored it.

To be clear, this wasn't something illegal or immoral, and it wasn't something I had heard from a concerned third party, or that I had observed personally. This was a conviction I had that the person concerned was wrestling with something.

I had a friendly work relationship with the person, but didn't know him that well, and yet what I thought I had received as a knowing seemed so out of character from what I *did* know of him.

The thing was, the more I ignored it, the stronger this conviction became. As I have already shared, I have learned over the years that often these knowings are divine nudges, and that it is at least worth registering them and waiting to see if God is wanting to say something.

'Lord,' I prayed. 'I need real wisdom from you about this. Firstly, about whether this is you speaking, and secondly what to do about it.'

Over the next few days two things happened – the first was that the knowing kept growing, each time with more detail, about what and when and also why. The second thing was that he seemed to be almost everywhere I went. Even in a big gathering, there he was, and he would catch my eye, almost like there was a big arrow hovering over him, pointing at his head.

'Okay, Lord, I get the message,' I prayed.

I knew that I needed to say something. I just didn't know how.

I talked it over with one of my mentors.

'Bill, I've only really got two pieces of advice.'

I leaned in.

'Remember that God hasn't told you this so that you can shame him. He's told you this because he loves this person. So much so that God doesn't want to leave him to his own devices. What you need to do is operate from a place of love. That must be your currency.'

He paused as I took in what he was saying. 'When it comes to difficult conversations, you only have authority with those who you love,' he smiled. 'Remember, it's not about you. You need to move past your discomfort. It's about providing space for God to reach out in love to this person.

'And secondly, be kind. You have carried this for a while. Don't be in a rush to get it over and done with – ask questions and give him time to absorb what you are saying.'

To my relief, when it came to the actual conversation, it went far better than I thought it might. My mentor's words, 'Let love be your currency,' were gently ringing in my ears.

TOUGH LOVE

In Chapter 12 I explained how the filter to put any prophetic word through is a series of questions about whether it is edifying, encouraging, reflecting the heart of Jesus and leading the person to a place where they will encounter the heart of the Father. And so, what do we do with a word of knowledge or prophetic word that appears more challenging than encouraging?

A few years ago, I had to do a sermon on one of the most challenging passages of Revelation, and as I was praying I said, 'Lord, it doesn't seem very encouraging.' God seemed to reply, *'Was the outcome a forgone conclusion? Because mercy triumphs over judgment.'*

When you read the letters to the seven churches, especially one that is more confrontational, like the one to the Church in Laodicea, it is hard to see them as encouraging.

> 'I know your deeds, that you are neither cold nor hot. I wish you were either one or the other! So, because you are lukewarm – neither hot nor cold – I am about to spit you out of my mouth. You say, "I am rich; I have acquired wealth and do not need a thing." But you do not realise that you are wretched, pitiful, poor, blind and naked.'
>
> REVELATION 3:15-18

This seems much more of a rebuke than encouragement. And yet, when you read on, just a few verses later you see the reason:

> 'Those whom I love I rebuke and discipline. So be earnest and repent.'
>
> REVELATION 3:19

---

* James 2:13.

And then follows one of the most encouraging and well-loved passages of scripture in the New Testament.

> 'Here I am! I stand at the door and knock. If anyone hears my voice and opens the door, I will come in and eat with that person, and they with me.'
>
> REVELATION 3:20

As I reflected on this, what I understood was that, actually, what can seem like the rebuke of an angry God is in fact the warning of a loving Father. When we look at Scripture, especially the Old Testament prophets, we see the number of times they warn the people of God about what could happen – when God could have just gone ahead and done it, allowed a calamity or disaster to happen, without confronting or warning them. You either believe that God is out to get people, or you believe in a God who is running towards people, waiting until the last possible moment, holding off judgment, calling to them, warning. '*If you don't turn around this is what'll happen, but you don't have to go down that road.*' That to me is the very definition of tough love.

OUT OF THE OVERFLOW

And the way you deliver a word, as we have already seen, can make all the difference. I have a very dear friend called Tim. In many ways he has been a combination of older brother, mentor and father figure to me since I met him nearly thirty years ago. Tim just loves encouraging people, and everyone he meets leaves feeling better for having spent time with him. He doesn't limit it to just people when he's at church, he does it everywhere he goes – the shopping mall, the drive-through, the gym.

He prophesies out of the overflow of who he is; he'll be with someone, and because his desire is to love and encourage everybody, he has cultivated the soil of his heart to such a degree that he doesn't go looking for people to encourage, it just happens wherever he is.

What I've noticed is that it moves from encouragement to the prophetic or words of knowledge naturally and easily, it's like a bubbling brook that overflows. I'm working to cultivate a heart of wanting to encourage everyone I meet, but I recognise for me I have to put a process in place. More than that, with people who aren't used to this, I have to approach that a little bit differently, because I have a tendency in myself to overthink and overcomplicate things, so therefore for me just deciding makes it easier and forces me to keep it simple.

YOU'RE BETTER THAN THIS

Our sons were playing in a football match. When the half-time whistle was blown, one mum called to her son and told him she'd brought him some water. He turned to her from twenty metres or so away and in particularly colourful language, more akin with the Fulham football fan in Chapter 2, told her to get lost.

She was understandably embarrassed and humiliated by the exchange. I felt desperately sorry for her, and to be honest my overriding emotion was sadness more than anything else. He was a friend of my son, and I had a relatively good relationship with him. I knew that what he had said had come out of embarrassment and also frustration at the way the game was going. In essence, what he had said didn't reflect who he was. I began to think how this situation might be turned around, how he could be the better version of himself I knew he was.

As it turned out the team turned the game around in the second half, and the boy who had been so rude to his mother played what the coach called 'an absolute blinder'. At the end of the match, I went and said well done to some of the players. I saw the boy on his own and walked up to him.

'Well played, mate,' I said to him with a big smile. 'You had a brilliant second half, which is why I was so surprised.'

'Surprised?' he asked.

'Ben,' I said to him, 'I guess I was a little surprised by what you said to your mum at half-time.'

Ben's head went down.

'You are such a leader. The team really look to you, and I guess the reason I was surprised is because what you said didn't reflect that. It kind of diminished you, and you are so much better than that. Anyway, as I said, well played; that goal you scored was absolutely phenomenal.'

'Thanks, Bill,' he said, still trying to work out what had just happened.

A few hours later I got a call from Ben's mother.

'Bill, I'm not sure what you said to Ben at the end of the game, but thank you.'

'No problem at all,' I responded.

'He got in the car, looked at me and said, "Mum, sorry for what I said at half-time. I know it was really rude and didn't make me look very good. I know I'm better than that, and my job as a leader in the team is to be better than that, so I'm really sorry."'

All I had done in that moment was to gently remind Ben who he was, and who he could be. I didn't mention God, I didn't offer to pray for him. Ben and his mother were both left feeling encouraged.

My conversation with Ben wasn't a particularly spiritual exchange, and only lasted about thirty seconds. While some may say that there wasn't anything particularly prophetic about it, I would argue that it was in some ways a great example of the prophetic; realigning someone's perspective of who they were with how God saw them, drawing out the gold, whether they realised it or not.

And although the word I gave to Ben could have been given and received as a rebuke, it was ultimately an encouraging word.

HANDLE WITH EXTRA CARE

> *'For I know the plans I have for you,'* declares the LORD, *'plans to prosper you and not to harm you, plans to give you hope and a future.'*
> JEREMIAH 29:11

This is an extraordinary promise. And God takes his promises seriously; he has a plan and a destiny for everyone – one that is permeated, overflowing, with hope.

And yet, I've learned that there are certain things that we just need to exercise extra special caution and wisdom and sensitivity around, no matter how prophetically gifted we might be. These include what are sometimes rather lightly termed 'hatches, matches and dispatches.' That is, struggling to conceive children, finding and choosing a life partner, and promises of healing to those who are terminally ill. These are deeply personal areas of people's lives – things that are close to people's hearts, and we need to remember that these things also matter deeply to God as well.

If you know a couple who have been married for a long time and haven't got children, of course your heart will be to love and encourage them. But that situation is so sensitive, pastorally speaking, that I would almost have to have God write a prophetic word in fire in the sky about anything to do with them having children before I would even consider sharing it. This is one of those times when it is doubly important to hold back a word until later, and to pray for the situation, pray and keep praying, and only when the time is right, which in my experience is after those prayers have been answered, to share it.

GOD SPEAKS IN A LONDON TAXI RIDE

I knew I was going to have to get a taxi if I wasn't going to be late. I hated being late – but on this occasion, as I stood at the bus stop with the digital display telling me that my next bus wasn't for another twenty-seven minutes, I wasn't sure what was frustrating me more

– the fact that I was running late or the fact that I was going to have to pay to be on time.

I stood on the Brompton Road scanning for taxis in the early evening traffic. It started to rain. 'Excellent,' I thought. 'Not only am I up against the clock, but I'm now going to get wet too.'

It seemed everyone else had had the same idea at the same time – I kept seeing taxis being hailed further down the road towards Knightsbridge. I checked my uber app – no luck there either. I sighed. If only I had been a bit more organised, I could have left earlier, and I wouldn't have found myself standing in the now pouring rain getting soaked as I tried to spot a taxi that was actually still for hire.

At that point, a taxi stopped ten or so metres away at the junction of Egerton Terrace and Brompton Road and turned its light on, then off again, then on again, then … I wasn't going to wait for it to be turned off again. I ran, knocked on the passenger window. 'Sorry, mate, I think I'm done for the day,' said the driver.

I sighed. 'No worries,' I replied. 'I couldn't work out if you were working or not.'

'Me neither,' replied the taxi driver.

'The good news is that it wasn't your lights on the blink!' I said. 'Excuse the terrible pun.'

He laughed and then paused. 'What way were you wanting to go?'

'Clapham North,' I replied. 'But don't worry – have a good evening.'

'Tell you what, mate, for making me laugh I'll take you there.'

'Are you sure?' I asked. 'I thought you were done for the day.'

'So did I – but it's on my way home, and it'll pay for my takeaway!' he said, smiling.

'You are, quite literally, a godsend,' I said as I got in. 'How long do you reckon it will take to get there?'

''Bout twenty-five minutes this time of day, I reckon,' the driver said without missing a beat.

'Perfect!' I replied. That would get me there with five minutes or so to spare. I sat back into my seat, breathed out and shook the rainwater off my jacket.

It was as we turned into Walton Street, out of nowhere a thought, a knowing, came into my mind, about the taxi driver, or rather, his wife. Initially I just let the thought linger – I didn't know anything about this man, or whether he had family of any kind, and I was also aware he had shown me a kindness in taking me when he was about to finish for the day.

The longer I let it linger, the stronger the thought became.

'Lord, is that you?' I asked. 'What do you want to talk to me about?'

A still, small voice in my inner ear replied, '*His wife.*'

I thought for a moment. While I had seen the driver's face when I was outside, now all I could see was the back of his head, and his eyes when he checked his rear-view mirror. That also wasn't a lot to go on, but, as with so many of the encounters I have had over the years, God tells us just enough, though not too much, to lead us where he wants to take us and the person we are with.

Often, with the prophetic, as with any conversation, I have learned to notice non-verbal cues. This isn't to try and second guess a response, but to see if what I am asking or saying is resonating. While this was admittedly easier than the conversation I had had with Simon on the phone at the McDonalds on the Wandsworth roundabout, I at least knew that during that conversation I had had Simon's full attention, and that we could both hear each other clearly. This was a little bit different – the driver was focussing on the road, and the intercom in a taxi isn't always all that good.

I'd learned over the years that it is better in these situations to be as open with initial questions as possible. The prophetic shouldn't ever leave anyone feeling like they've been hustled, pushed, violated or manipulated in any way. It should be the most positive, life-giving experience they have had that day. It should leave them knowing that God is good, that he knows them, that they really matter to him and that he loves them. All too often it is easy to be in such a rush to share what we believe God has shared with us that we end up not taking the time to wait and see what else God might want to reveal to us, charging on into a situation before we are ready and forgetting the person we are speaking to.

'Has it been a busy day?' I asked.

'Crazy.'

'Crazy good, or crazy bad?'

'Just crazy. I've been here, there and everywhere. London, days like today, the traffic being what it is … '

'Yep, I know what you mean. It drives my wife mad sometimes.'

'Yeah?'

'She's not a Londoner – she's learned to like it, but I think she would far rather we lived somewhere else with more space.'

I paused.

'Do you have family?' I asked.

'I do, mate, I do. And I know what your wife means. My missus is the same.'

There was something, a tone, in his voice as he mentioned his wife. As he said it, that gentle whisper spoke to my inner ear again, '*She's very ill.*' As I heard the words, in my mind's eye I saw a lady lying in a darkened room with blue walls and cream-coloured curtains. She looked gaunt and pale. As I allowed the picture to settle more details came into focus. I have found that this is often the case when I see these pictures in my mind's eye, or as more overt open visions. It can be easy to take the initial revelation and run with that, rather than giving God the time to slowly reveal the details – much like the polaroid photograph example.

'I hope you don't mind me asking,' I said tentatively. 'And I don't want to intrude in any way, and if you'd rather not talk about it, I totally understand … but I get the sense that your wife might be ill?' I asked gently.

The driver looked at me curiously through the mirror.

'Mate, if you only knew … ' I could hear the sadness in his voice.

The voice in my inner ear again, full of compassion and concern, a gentle whisper, revealed more – giving context to the detail in the picture I had allowed to settle in my mind's eye.

'Do you mind me asking your name?' I inquired.

'Brian.'

'Brian, I know we've never met before, and that I'm just some random bloke who got into your cab at the end of your shift, and if you'd rather drop me off here that's totally fine. I know it's hard right now, in all the pain, fear and confusion you are feeling. I can't even begin to imagine how hard it must be watching your wife struggle and try fighting the cancer as she lies in a darkened room with blue walls, but you are not alone, your wife is not alone … '

He looked at me in the mirror again, his eyes a mixture of confusion and surprise.

'Mate, are you sure we haven't met before?'

'I'm pretty sure.'

Brian pulled the taxi to the side of the road and turned round and looked at me. 'How did you know that? About my wife? About the cancer? About the colour of the walls in the hospice – she only moved in there yesterday?' His voice cracking with emotion. 'Do you work in the hospice or something?'

'My name is Bill. I'm a vicar.'

'Rev … ' said Brian, and with that he got out of the driver's seat, opened the back passenger door, got in and sat opposite me, his eyes now red and full of tears. He pulled a photo of him and his wife out of his wallet. 'This is us on holiday last year. In happier times. She's beautiful, isn't she?'

I looked at the photo – they looked so happy, so blissfully unaware of what was to come. 'She is,' I replied.

'Why is this happening? Why is this happening to her? She's never done anything wrong. She doesn't deserve this, and how come you know what you do?'

'Brian, I don't know why this is happening. I am so, so sorry for what you and your wife are experiencing,' I said slowly. 'I believe that often God reaches out to people when they are in the darkest places, because they matter to him, because their pain matters to him, to let them know that he is with them, and that they are not alone.'

'Rev, can I tell you something?' Brian asked.

I nodded.

'I was driving around today just thinking, what's the point? When Sue dies, what's the point of carrying on, you know?'

I nodded. 'Brian, I know nothing I can say is going to take away your pain, but I really believe that God wants to meet you and be with you and carry you when you feel like you can't carry on.'

Brian was sobbing now; big, deep, raw moans of sadness and grief. I could feel the tears rolling down my own cheeks too. We sat there for a while, my hand on his shoulder, the windows of the taxi increasingly covered in condensation.

We talked some more, and then he got back in the front of the cab, and we made our way to Clapham North. We sat and talked for a few more minutes, I prayed for him, gave him my number and said he could call anytime if he wanted to talk. He refused to take any money for the ride.

'What about your takeaway?' I asked.

'I've got more than enough to take away from that ride to last me a while. Thanks again, Rev,' he said, before pulling out from the kerb, waving out of the window and disappearing into the evening traffic.

Ten days later I got a call on my phone. 'Rev, this is Brian – the taxi driver ... I just wanted you to know that Sue died yesterday. I told her about your taxi journey when I got to the hospice that evening. It brought her real comfort ... What you said helped us and gave us hope in these last few days.'

Sometimes there just isn't a happy ending, we can't promise healing or a miracle, but just knowing that God is there, he loves us, and he cares, can be all the help in the world.

afterword

This book is, at its core, a story about a friendship. Captivated by an American pastor's talk in a London church just over thirty years ago, it tells some of the stories, as best I can remember, of what has happened as I have sought, often falteringly, to know in my own life what it might mean to be a friend of God. I still have a long way to go. I am closer than I was, but the shore is still far off and on clear days I can just about make out its shape across the sea in the distance.

I did not start my journey back then knowing what prophecy was, and even when I did learn what it was, I have tried not to make it my focus.

What I haven't shared until now is that God came closest, and I began to encounter his presence and his heart on a daily basis at a time in my life that I least expected, during a season when plans and hopes and dreams in many ways seemed to be falling apart. I was dealing with the fallout of a situation, which although I knew was right, had left me broken and I wasn't sure if I wanted to stay in full-time Christian ministry at all. To be honest there were moments when I wasn't sure I wanted to be a follower of Jesus anymore.

It was the kindness and generosity of the pastors at that same London church I found myself in thirty years previously, who offered me a job at this time, that helped me begin to recover. I was reminded again as I looked around the church of all the times and places in that building where I had encountered God and heard his voice so often in the past.

It was there, when all I really wanted to do was hide, that God, in his kindness, began to speak to me in that gentle whisper, in ways I had not experienced before, to share his heart with me in ways that called me out of my hiddenness into a new and deeper friendship with him. Here, he began to speak to me as a friend in ways that I never could have imagined, that invited me to:

'Arise … come with me.
See! The winter is past;
  the rains are over and gone.
Flowers appear on the earth;
  the season of singing has come.'
SONG OF SONGS 2:10-13

Prophecy, as we have seen, is by nature deeply relational.

Relationships take time, and the ones that mean the most will have periods where the friendships are deepened and enriched by time spent together and memories are made. The same is true of our relationship with God.

There will be seasons in our lives when God will continually amaze us, where we walk closely with him, knowing his presence and encountering his voice as he shares his heart with us for ourselves and also for other people.

Just as I have shared some of these moments in this book, if you let him, if you search for him, if you have the courage to let him lead you and speak to you, you will find him writing a book with you of your own stories of people whose lives you have had the extraordinary privilege of stepping into at just the right moment, of people encountering the love and goodness of God for the first time, often in the most surprising and unusual places, at times you least expect.

There will also be times when he is quieter. I am learning that those are often the times when he is doing the deeper work in us. Resting us, shaping us, forming us. Although it may feel like it, this is not passive on his part.

Just over two years ago I found myself in a season when the Lord seemed quieter, where his presence was less tangible and he was not sharing his heart for others with me in the way that I had been experiencing previously. It was unsettling in some ways. I was on my favourite walk one late November morning, across what, during the summer, had been a maize field. The ground was firm beneath my feet from the frost. 'Lord, what is going on? How come I'm not encountering your presence and your heart for people as I have done in the past?' I asked.

Slowly a gentle whisper came, '*Look at the field … What do you see?*'

'A field with stalks where the maize was before the harvest in August,' I answered.

'*And what is happening in the field now?*'

'Nothing.'

'*Nothing is ever nothing. Look again. The frost would have killed the maize. The field is being rested. And as it is being rested, it is recovering. Slowly, even as it seems that nothing is going on, the field is getting ready for life to return, so that when the time is right it will be ready for fresh seed to be planted and grown, ready for a new crop. Ready for another harvest. And what is true for this field is true for your soul, if you embrace the season I have led you into.*'

I stopped and took the scene in. Although it seemed lifeless, it took on a new beauty as I thought about those words.

Over the next few months, I pondered those words often, spoken by a Father to a son. I learned to embrace the season, unsettling as it was at times. As I did, I began to see him at work deep in my soul – refreshing, restoring, and at times refining. He was never in a rush, always attentive, and his work in me ever more real as I walked those fields.

Since God led me out of that season, I have encountered his presence in deep and profound moments and known a depth of friendship and intimacy with him that I did not know was possible. I am still far from the shore, but I am slowly edging closer. I have witnessed him work in some of the most extraordinary ways, in the most unusual places with some of the most unlikely people.

Those are perhaps stories for another time.

Muddy
Pearl